GIL HOGG

TEACHING YOURSELF TRANQUILLITY

MEDITATION WITHOUT MANTRAS

LOTUS
BOOKS

LOTUS BOOKS
7 Old Estate Yard
Normanby
Scunthorpe DN15 9JA, UK
Email: admin@lotusbooks.co.uk
Web: www.lotusbooks.co.uk

Design and distribution:
Matador Publishing
9 De Montfort Mews
Leicester LE1 7FW, UK
Email: books@troubador.co.uk
Web: www.troubador.co.uk/matador

ISBN 1 904744 69 9

Cover illustration: Rod Clark

Typeset in 11pt Stempel Garamond by
Troubador Publishing Ltd, Leicester, UK

Printed by The Cromwell Press Ltd, Trowbridge, Wilts, UK

TEACHING
YOURSELF TRANQUILLITY

MEDITATION WITHOUT MANTRAS

BY THE SAME AUTHOR
A Smell of Fraud
The Predators

CONTACT THE AUTHOR AT
admin@lotusbooks.co.uk
or ask him to speak to your
organisation

CONTENTS

v

TWENTY MINUTES OF NOTHING
IN YOUR DIARY

If I tell you that meditation in its simplest form is concentration on a fixed point with a clear mind, you'll probably say, "Look at my schedule for the day! Look at my worry list! A blank mind? You're crazy!"

I know, you have a million things to do, and think about, and I'm asking you to put twenty minutes of nothing in your diary – every day. What are you going to write down on the page to remind yourself? Perhaps *Teaching Yourself Tranquillity* (15 mins), or maybe just *Doing nothing, zero, zilch*. Every day a twenty-minute slot, or five minutes, if that's all you have, of ... nothing.

You've tried this before, haven't you? And it doesn't work. Peace, calm, bells dinging, candles, all that stuff. It sounds good, but it isn't really practical. You ask, how can anybody devote twenty minutes, or even five minutes, to a total blank? Your head is supposed to be calm! Hell, it's crawling with anxieties. How can anybody in their right mind write on their To-Do List, *Doing nothing* (10 mins)? Time's too precious, isn't it?

What you're really saying is that you prefer to go on stumbling from task to task, from the first worry on your list, to the next. You don't have time to work out what's going on around you. The day is a succession of must-dos, getting out of bed when the alarm rings, grabbing some toast, running for the train, meetings at work, shopping, cooking, paying bills, picking up the kids in the car, visiting your mother. There's no way out, and no let up. How could you possibly justify doing nothing for a few minutes every day? And let's face it, a lot of these things don't put a smile on your face. They're downright miserable or kind of unsatisfactory.

Wait a minute. Do you seriously mean you haven't got time to understand about yourself? You haven't got time to create tranquillity in the hustle of everyday life? You haven't got time to work out that in this case, nothing is really a very big something? *Teaching Yourself Tranquillity* isn't about lying under a sunshade on the beach. It's about solving your problems every day in a way that's most useful or enjoyable to you. So that little entry, *Teaching Myself Tranquillity* (10 mins), in your To-Do List, is actually a very big deal.

A meditation colleague of mine was one of the busiest people I know. She was living with a guy whom she loved, who already had two young kids who weren't easy, and holding down a creative job in an advertising agency – the sort of job where you sometimes meet with clients before breakfast, or finish at midnight. She was lover, mother, housekeeper, and career woman. I said to her one day, after she had been meditating a while, "How are you finding the time?", and she replied, "It's because I meditate that I have the time, and the cool, to cope with the mad-house. When I first moved in with Bob and the boys, it was hell. Everything I did, even in bed, seemed to happen on the run. In the first few months I thought that much as I love Bob, I couldn't go on. There was too much hustle and bustle for it to be a pleasure. Then I met you, and began to meditate. I saw that I'd got it all wrong. At work and at home, I had been rushing from crisis to crisis. Now I'm moving easily between the duties I have to do, and the people I love. If we run out of cereal, or I'm held up at a late meeting, it isn't a crisis any more."

Alice had worked out that the aggravation isn't worth it, if you can't enjoy. And she also saw that Bob and the boys didn't need to change. They were having a ball. Her problems weren't their fault. Alice had to change. She had to cool it, and get a little tranquillity into her attitude. That's where *Teaching Yourself Tranquillity* comes in. Personal meditation is what you do when you sit or walk quietly. Living Meditation is what you do every day when you confront a problem and solve it.

These two practices don't take very long to learn, and they have a big payoff – enjoyment of life. Alice, who was really depressed when I first met her, is now managing a stressful life with enjoyment. It's not magic. It's taking a realistic look at the way things are.

Most of us are pushed around by our mind as it

responds to all the pressures and anxieties of the day. The mind jumps around like a monkey in the forest. We need to focus calmly and get our thinking right. I mean the kind of thinking that sorts out the problem in the most sensible way, and allows us to enjoy life. When Alice is racing home in a cab at nine at night, having missed dinner because a meeting drizzled on, she knows it's simply stressful to get het up about Bob and the boys. She's calm. Getting uptight would just be taking an additional burden on herself. This is what *Teaching Yourself Tranquillity* is all about, using personal meditation and Living Meditation to solve our problems. Why shouldn't we get as much enjoyment as possible out of everything we do?

IF YOU FEEL HASSLED

This book is for you – and me. We're stressed by our busy job or studies, and coping with family, colleagues, friends, traffic, public transport, the internet and every damn event that's going on. Maybe we have a lot of plus things in our world, but it feels pressured and unsatisfactory.

We need to get quality into our lives, and have some fun at the same time. It isn't easy. If we're disabled or bereaved we have to come to terms with it. And that's a lot harder.

PUT YOUR LUGGAGE IN THE RACK AND RELAX

We are often like the man who struggles on to a train with a heavy suitcase. The suitcase is heavy because it contains every problem the man has. The train leaves the station, and begins to rattle along like our lives. But the man hasn't put the suitcase down on the floor of the carriage or in the rack! We sometimes hold on to the suitcase, and support it for the entire journey. We need to learn to let go.

QUICK FIXES WON'T DO IT

I'm going to tell you in simple terms how to free your life from stress, and enjoy it more, or come to terms with serious loss. I can teach you how to do this because I did it myself, and it works. *Teaching Yourself Tranquillity* is about helping you deal effectively with the frustrations, disappointment, sorrow and anger which are part of our daily lives. It's a path that's healthy, cheap and has long-term effects.

An accountant friend of mine suffering from tension at work recently went on an expensive spa weekend, and I met him in the street afterwards. "How was it?" I asked. "Great," he said. "Like staying at the Ritz. And I've lost weight, got a good diet, and I'm back to the gym." I ran into him in his office six weeks later, and he wasn't looking so good. "I thought you were back on track," I said. "Well, not really," Alec replied. "I've got a new boss, and my youngest daughter hasn't been so well – but that's the way it is, I guess." Actually, life doesn't have to be this disappointing.

The problem with Alec's quick fix at a spa was that it didn't last, any more than the glow from alcohol, or the high from a pill. *Teaching Yourself Tranquillity* has the answer because it is a way of living, not a fix. After all the physical exercise and pampering with mineral baths, diets, aromatherapy and massage, life will always be difficult – and therefore you end up back at square one.

NO BELLS, CANDLES OR THERAPIES

Meditation often comes in a sermon from a guru, or in a medical wrapper from a psychotherapist. I am teaching it to you on the basis that it is something the ordinary person can use, without the mysticism or medicine bit. *Teaching Yourself Tranquillity* doesn't have any spiritual or moral messages. Perhaps you jog or go to the gym a couple of times a week. That's exercise for the body. What about exercise for the mind? Calming and clearing your mind, and moving on to useful thoughts can enhance your abilities, as well as increase your enjoyment of life.

SIMPLY RELIEVE STRESS, OR OPT FOR THE WHOLE NINE YARDS

Personal meditation is simple to learn, and leads in a practical and logical way to a different way of dealing with life. You can use it, if you want, merely as an exercise to relieve stress, and bring a little calm and relaxed enjoyment to your life. You don't have to follow through with a different way of dealing with life. That's the Living Meditation part. It's your choice. I guarantee, however, that if you decide to follow *Teaching Yourself Tranquillity*, whichever option you choose, you'll find two things fairly quickly. First, you'll notice the benefit right from the start. And second, you'll appreciate the benefit enough to make it a regular part of your day.

Before moving to the why and how of meditation, let me briefly tell you my story.

MY STORY

I discovered meditation over ten years ago. I was a successful lawyer, and a top corporate executive with a good marriage and two great kids. But life didn't taste right. I had always thought once I got these things, the wanting and striving would be over, and I'd be happy, but it didn't work out that way.

I had a big job and I took it seriously. Life wasn't funny. I didn't laugh much. I had a million worries – nothing I couldn't handle, but enough to make me reach for a notepad when I woke up at three o'clock in the morning. My marriage and children were in second place. My days were all scheduled. I was impatient, always urging others to get on with it. Traffic jams and slow talkers drove me crazy. There was a deadline urgency about everything I did. I was still striving, and competing – for what? That's what I ultimately asked myself. Why was life unsatisfactory if I had everything I'd aimed for?

It was a time when meditation was flavour of the month with corporate executives, to help enhance performance. With hardly a thought, I lined up for my dose, as I had for all the past self-improvement gimmicks. And it worked! This exercise actually had a calming effect, and improved my concentration. I found I was more effective at my job, and I actually began to enjoy life!

But I wasn't quite sure what I'd bought. Yes, it worked as an exercise. But it was surrounded by a lot of mystical and spiritual stuff that was quite simply unexplained. I kept asking myself, and my teachers, "Yes, but why?" From those who were Buddhists, I got the answer according to their religion; from those who weren't, I didn't get anything very satisfactory. I began to study the Buddhist religion. I attended retreats. I met and learned from many gurus. I also read widely about meditation, and listened to some of the many non-Buddhists and quasi-Buddhists who teach it. I saw that meditation plays a part in Judaism and Christianity.

The result? I wasn't a Buddhist. I felt a profound respect for the religion. I couldn't be a half-Buddhist, picking out the bits of it that I liked, and rejecting the rest. And I didn't want to have any mystical ceremony or theory that I didn't understand and believe in. So I developed the personal meditation and Living Meditation which are the foundations of *Teaching Yourself Tranquillity*, based on simple facts and human psychology we all know and understand.

So a personal quest for understanding has become

a book. I had already published a couple of novels, and I thought I should turn to the most important piece of non-fiction for me – how to get the benefits and knowledge I have across to other people in a clear way. I was troubled, from my research and from meetings with other meditators, about the "spiritual" and "ethical" claims that were made for meditation, outside of established religions. How could spiritual values follow from a simple exercise in concentration? I thought there was something misleading here, pulled out of the air to impress people, and give meditation a spurious kind of solemnity. That's why *Teaching Yourself Tranquillity* is easy and logical, and has no bells, candles, mantras or transcendental paths.

1

THE WHAT, WHY, AND HOW OF IT

WHAT PERSONAL AND LIVING MEDITATION CAN DO FOR YOU

This is really a summary of points I'm going to enlarge on.

Meditation is a special kind of exercise. Just as lifting weights in the gym is exercise for our arms, so meditation is exercise for our mind. Lifting weights strengthens the arm muscles; meditation strengthens the mind muscles. We take with us, from personal meditation, into daily life, and Living Meditation, not only an appreciation of calm, but the ability to focus on helpful thoughts. All too often we are the captive of a stream of impressions without really being conscious of what is happening around us. What we have been doing in personal meditation, is to develop the ability to think the thoughts we want to think, and put aside the rest.

We know that we live *exclusively* in the quality of our thoughts. Think nasty or confused thoughts, and we'll be having a depressing time. If we are full of anger and hate, we suffer the pain and anxiety of those feelings. If we think helpful thoughts, we'll be having a good time. If we feel calm and peace, we can enjoy the moment.

Relieving stress
Improving concentration
Living in the present and understanding it
more
Coping with change
Understanding ourselves
Living in harmony with events around us
Acceptance of difficult situations
Enhancing our enjoyment
Avoiding pessimism

RELIEVING STRESS

Stress permeates our lives. Stress at work and stress in relationships. We are forever trying to meet the expectations and standards set by other people; our employer, our coach, our family, our friends. Personal meditation can give us the focus to see that stress is our reaction. The only "reality" stress has is inside our head. It's a self-imposed burden, which we can shed, if we have the right perspective on it.

IMPROVING CONCENTRATION

Personal meditation helps us to cultivate the state of mind we need to deal with whatever situation we find ourselves in. Living Meditation enables us to put it into action. We need to be able to concentrate on the thoughts and emotions that are constructive at any particular moment in everyday life. This habit of concentration carries through to all the tasks we have to perform, at work, at home, at school, at leisure, in sport. We perform better and enjoy it more.

Because we put all our difficulties aside when we're in personal meditation, every moment of concentration during a session, is practice for focusing our thoughts later in Living Meditation. The more often we lay our habitual thoughts and worries aside, the less habitual and worrisome they become. We are much better able to bring a relaxed mind to focus on the tasks of every day.

LIVING IN THE PRESENT AND UNDERSTANDING IT MORE

Meditation can help us to live in the present. How much time do we waste regretting the past, and worrying or hoping about the future? Life is not happening in the past. That's memory. It's not happening in the future either, because we haven't got there yet. That's dreaming. All we have is the present, and although it seems absurd, because we already know it, we have to learn how to use this knowledge, because it is the only way we can be truly happy.

Julia is a friend of mine in her thirties with everything going for her – good health, good looks, and a satisfying job, but she isn't coping with life very gracefully. Her partner left her a few months ago, and since then she has lived in a state of perpetual regret and recrimination. She really feels her life "ended" when her partner let her down. She's a very nice woman, but she has allowed the past to poison the present. And I expect you have met people like Carol, a young married woman I know, who can't rest unless she has planned and scheduled every aspect of tomorrow for herself, her husband and her children. No occasion ever really lives up to Carol's expectations. She lives for tomorrow. She has a fixed vision of what is supposed to happen, and of course, as we know, things usually turn out differently. Neither Julia nor Carol are living in the here and now, at all.

Personal meditation and Living Meditation can give us the perspective to see that the past and the future, important as they are, are not life. Life is now, this moment.

COPING WITH CHANGE

In order to enjoy the present, we need to see it is always changing. We are not the same person we were yesterday. And change isn't limited to birth, growth, decay and death in living creatures. The fact of constant change in the physical world, and in every piece of matter within it, is one of the wonders of our existence. The change may be imperceptible, but it is there. We would like to think, and sometimes do, that things and people are permanent, solid, and unchanging. We talk about "things as they are", but it's an illusion. Everything is changing, all the time, and in every moment. Things can never be as they were yesterday.

When my marriage to my first wife ended,

she used to say to me critically, "You've changed!", as though we had some kind of deal that I would or could remain the same. I could only reply, "Yes, that's the problem." I wasn't the same person she'd married nearly a decade earlier – how could I have been?

We therefore need to understand the significance of change in our lives. It means that we have to cope with the unexpected. It means we cannot predict what will happen. Most important, if means we are often disappointed at the way our wishes, and our plans, turn out. Personal meditation and Living Meditation can give us the calm and balance to live in a changing present.

UNDERSTANDING OURSELVES

Personal meditation enables us to see that our success and enjoyment of life is based on *our perceptions*. Everything starts with us, personally. We each have to take responsibility for what we think and do, and it therefore makes sense to think and do the things that make us happy. If we blame others for our problems, we find that we suffer frustration and disappointment.

A client of mine used to have an almost continual frown, and a very tense mouth. Alan was a hard man to please, because, in his view he never made a mistake. All his troubles were down to other people, and he spent a good deal of his time cursing and complaining about them. Whenever we had a business crisis that I knew he had contributed to, I used to wait to hear him tell it otherwise. It was him against the world, and it showed. I always felt that Alan never took a good look at himself, never understood that the biggest cause of his problems was the misery of his own anger and disappointment.

In Living Meditation we become conscious of the misleading effect of our own, often fanciful view of ourselves; the "I am" approach, the vision of "my rights," "my property," "my reputation." The delusion that people ought to treat us in a certain way, because of whom we think we are, can be a very painful one, which we need to learn to avoid. We begin to understand that the big "I am" is an illusion, and we feel more comfortable with ourselves.

LIVING IN HARMONY WITH EVENTS AROUND US

If we are conscious of the tide of change, we see that it's stronger than we are. The only question is whether we struggle painfully against the tide, or go with it. If we go with it, this doesn't mean we'll never say no, and never protest. There may be a time when we have to stand up against others for what we believe. There will be lots of occasions when we have to make our point. What accepting change means is that we will observe the flow of events around us in a new way – with detachment. Instead of being uptight at the way life is treating us, instead of getting angry, and frustrated by events we can't

9

control, we'll view things calmly. We'll realise that all that's happening when we get depressed or upset or angry is that we are imposing grief on ourselves. When things turn out badly, we'll be able ride them with the thought, *This is just a happening, like the wind or the rain, and there's no more sense in getting mad, than there would be sense in getting mad at the weather.*

ACCEPTANCE OF DIFFICULT SITUATIONS

I appreciate that you're thinking, *It's all very well to talk about calm in the ordinary run of daily life, but there are some events like wars, genocide, murder, and personal injury or loss, that you can't expect me to take easily.* You're right. We not only have to view change calmly, but we sometimes have to accept what is virtually unacceptable. Living Meditation can help with a different perspective on acceptance.

We understand that we are going to be

buffeted around in the course of our lives. However we try to shelter, death, illness, serious injury and crime reach out to affect us. The event can be horrifying, enough to disturb even the most placid and detached of us. When the initial shock has passed, we strive to place our feelings and our actions on the useful side of the ledger – that is, with calm and tolerance, rather than anger and anguish. Shall we say we try to keep them on the white path, rather than the gray path? If we don't succeed in this, difficult though it is, we suffer grievous and unnecessary pain.

ENHANCING OUR ENJOYMENT OF LIFE

Sensual pleasures like eating and drinking are short-lived. If we overdo them, they cease to be pleasant. Life unfortunately isn't one long orgasm, and in truth is full of dissatisfactions. When we develop the focus of mind, through Living Meditation, that enables us to live in the present, we'll genuinely enjoy what we do, rather than be comparing

11

how important, or unimportant, it is in relation to what somebody else is doing. We
won't be looking over the fence all the time.
What we enjoy, we tend to do well, and we'll
find our abilities are enhanced in many
respects, by the confidence that we are giving
our tasks our best shot.

AVOIDING PESSIMISM

Sometimes healthy, and outwardly "happy"
people, feel that things are not right, that life
has lost its sharpness and taste in an indefin-
able way; they find life unsatisfactory without being able to define precisely why. And
of course a great many more people suffer
from loneliness, stress, depression, physical
pain, illness, disablement and want. Why is
life so often anything from unsatisfactory to
downright painful? Why, even for people
who have a lot of good fortune, is life so
often gray?

We know the obvious answers – because we

are under pressure from family or friends, or our employer, or our community. Or because we're broke, or ill, or born with a disability, or we have a drug habit we can't kick. Or because our personal relationships aren't going well, or the children are playing up. Or because we desperately need something we can't afford, or we didn't get that promotion at work. Or because of plain bad luck. And so it goes on. *Hey, wait a minute! This is how life actually is, every day!*

We can't enjoy life unless we understand how life is *every day.* Living Meditation brings the insight to overcome the disappointment factor, and relieve that feeling of helplessness and pessimism; it opens us to calm acceptance of the way things are. We decide we're going to enjoy, and then we can enjoy.

HOW PERSONAL MEDITATION WORKS

I'm going to explain *how it works* quite shortly, then - at last – we'll come to the *how to do it.*

RELAXING INTO THE PRESENT MOMENT

In personal meditation, the mind is not calmed by any forceful or strained technique, but by letting go of anxiety about the past and the future, and relaxing into the present. The present – when we're meditating – will be a tranquil moment, because if we can, we have chosen a quiet time and place. It's as though we're saying, *I'm John Smith, and I'm here, and it's now.* All our life so far, our loves and hates, failures and successes, have come to this calm moment. We may have fought with the SAS, been a pop star, or a cook, but for each of us, life is just this tranquil moment, and no more. The past is gone. The future hasn't happened. There is only now. Perfect peace.

We find that there is something attractive about this simple creation of peace.

It sounds quite simple, and it is, but it requires practice. What we will be doing in personal meditation is getting constant practice in switching off worries about the past, and desires for the future – it's the only way to clear our head. We abandon our thoughts as we come to the *now*, as though they were passing clouds on a windy day. We realise that our thoughts, a fair proportion of which are trivial and nonsensical, are just thoughts, they are not "reality."

We feel lighter. We are in a calm state. We are here, and it is now.

What we want to do is to maintain that calm state while we are sitting, and to help us to do this, we gently place our attention on the breath in the vicinity of the tip of our nose. I'll say more about this when I discuss *How to do it.*

HOW IT WORKS AFTER PERSONAL MEDITATION

When we go about our daily business, we take that feeling of calm with us. Of course it doesn't last forever, and that's why we try to meditate at least once a day if we can. It's a good feeling, and some people may feel that's all they want, some ease and release from stress.

HOW IT WORKS IN LIVING MEDITATION

Living Meditation is the second phase. We use exactly the same model as personal meditation – we focus on the moment we have to deal with, the now, putting aside cares about the past and worries about tomorrow. It's our daily life so we don't create a space of peace as we did when we were sitting. Instead, we confront the problem we have, realising that it is generated by the inevitability of change. There is (1) the problem, and (2) our reaction to it. We can't, in all probability, make the problem go away, but we can react to it in the way most helpful and least painful to us. It's the same for small problems and big ones – the garden shed needs a new roof; or a very good friend is seriously ill. Living Meditation deals with how we accept the inevitable, and minimise the "I want" factor; how we fit most comfortably and enjoyably into the reality of our changing lives.

HOW PERSONAL AND LIVING MEDITATION GO TOGETHER

In personal meditation, we are constantly noticing the quality of our thoughts because, although our attention is on our breath, thoughts keep drifting back to us. We note them, and abandon them gently, in favour of the peace of the moment. Some thoughts are trivial and easy to let go; others are more serious – but they are merely thoughts. They are not "reality". They may have to be dealt with later, when we face the problem they represent. This awareness of the quality of our thoughts goes with us when we are in the street doing our business. Personal meditation, practised regularly, heightens the awareness. Personal meditation energises Living Meditation. Because we sit, we are more conscious of the importance of living in the moment in our daily lives, more conscious of the inevitability of change, and more conscious of the harmful effect on us, of a lot of our wishes and desires.

Personal meditation and Living Meditation work in sequence. I have a friend, George, who used to accompany me to the occasional retreat. He picked up meditation very quickly and found it beneficial, but one day he said to me, "I don't have any problem with accepting the inevitability of change, and reducing my ego a bit to enable me to be detached, but I find the personal meditation difficult. It doesn't suit me. Anyway, I think I can apply meditative awareness in daily life without actually sitting." When I saw George a few months later, and asked him how he was managing without actually sitting in meditation, he said, "I have to admit that Living Meditation is in my good ideas bag, with all the other good ideas, and I don't get around to applying meditative awareness as much as I should." The simple fact is that unless we get into the habit of awareness through personal meditation, it becomes harder and harder to focus meditative awareness on our problems in daily life. Living Meditation becomes a neglected "good idea" instead of a way of life.

GETTING READY TO DO IT

DO I NEED MY KAFTAN AND BEADS FOR THIS?

No, it doesn't matter what we wear, but it's helpful to wear something unrestricting and comfortable.

We need to find as quiet a place as possible where we can sit down. Quiet is sometimes hard to find, and we may have to meditate on occasions with background noise. It doesn't matter.

We can sit in a chair – that's fine. Or we can sit on the floor with our legs crossed. There isn't any magic in sitting on a cushion with our legs crossed like a child in kindergarten; it can be a posture some find natural for this exercise. If our legs are stiff, we don't cross them! We can use a cushion on the floor; this isn't intended to be a hardship. Or we can try sitting on our bed, cross legged or otherwise.

We ought to be poised, so our trunk is upright without strain. If we can only achieve this by resting our back against a wall, that's all right. If we're on our bed, we can use the bedhead.

We rest our hands in front of us, allow our head to bend very slightly forward. Our head shouldn't be laid back, because this is inclined to produce tension. Whatever position we adopt, we try to have our head and upper body resting easily so that we can forget about them. We don't want our attention to stray to the discomforts of the body. *But in the end, any upright posture we can take up, which removes strain from our shoulders, back and limbs, will serve.*

When we've been sitting for a few minutes, tension may creep back into our shoulders, neck and limbs. We will need to consciously relax ourselves from time to time.

Why have the trunk upright? Because we don't want to go off to sleep! We're aiming to be sharply awake. We can meditate lying down on a couch or bed, but the relaxation is so complete that sleep will tend to come. Some people who have trouble sleeping, start to meditate to encourage sleep. There's no harm and considerable benefit in doing this – if your aim is sleep.

Ready?

What about the candles, and the incense I brought back from Katmandu? You don't *need* any paraphernalia to meditate. There's nothing wrong at all in setting up an environment which suits you, but remember, this isn't a religious or spiritual ceremony. It's an exercise. In itself it has nothing to do with moral or ethical values (although it's true that you may make decisions in Living Meditation which fit in with moral and ethical values). Therefore, I wouldn't recommend any props; no candles, no incense, no bells. If you travel around the town and country or abroad regularly, you'll want to meditate in all sorts of places. It's best to get used to meditating, wherever you happen to be, without any aids. Complete simplicity is the key.

HOW TO DO IT

We're nearly there, and as I said, it's simple but not easy.

We consciously relax in our posture, putting our mind first on the forehead, and then running down the body: cheeks, jaw, shoulders, arms, legs.

The next step is to close the mouth, and breathe through the nose (if you can't breathe through your nose, don't worry). We close our eyes. We have a sense of seeing in the dark – all sorts of shadows and shapes. We can feel our breath rising and falling. We stay like that for a few moments, following the breath, in and out, and quietly confirming that we are *here*, and it is *now*. We have dedicated this time, be it five minutes or thirty, to meditation.

THE BREATH-POINT

Now, we place our attention on the point, in the vicinity of the tip of our nose, where the breath first touches the nose as we breathe in. Often, there is a slightly cool sensation there, caused by the cool air touching the membrane of the nose, as it is drawn into the lungs. We bring our attention as closely as we can to this point where the breath first touches the nose. We try to hold the point with our full attention. We don't strain.

We want to become conscious of the nature of our breath at this point. Is it deep or short? Slow or quick? We don't try to change it, but simply be aware, holding our attention steadily on that cool spot, which I will call the "breath-point." Incidentally, if the point isn't cool, so be it! It's still the point where the incoming breath touches the nostril. And if you're bothered about the precise point, let's just say the point is the tip of your nose.

CONSCIOUSNESS OF THE BREATH

The movement of the breath is secondary to our attention on the breath-point. We simply notice the breath – deep and slow, or shallow, a mere tremor. And we notice it *at the breath-point*, where the breath first touches the nose.

We want to keep the breath-point, on which we're concentrated, as small as possible. It's easier to fix our attention on a small point, rather than a wider area. We know the breath travels quite a distance after it touches the nose. It goes down into the lungs, expanding the chest, and then it's expelled. We are not thinking of this long journey made by the breath. Our attention is limited to the small point where the indrawn and exhaled breath touches the nose, the breath-point.

The breath is involuntary. It's what our body requires, not what we decide. We don't try to get a rhythmic rise and fall of the breath going. We become aware that as we proceed, and we are completely relaxed, our breath slows.

We simply focus our attention exclusively on the breath-point. *Exclusively*. It is the positive attraction of the breath-point that holds us, whatever is happening in our mind, beyond it. It is the centre of peace and calm.

LOSING THE BREATH-POINT

I expect your natural reaction to this is to say, *If that's all there is to it, I'm sure I can do it very easily.* Good, but you will find you can't concentrate for more than a few seconds on the breath-point – yes, a few seconds. Thoughts nudge us, and we imagine clouds obscuring the breath-point, we drift away from it.

We lose the breath-point, and we have to try to find it again. The clouds are a normal event. They have nothing to do with meditation. If we close our eyes at any time, after a while we can see moving shapes. These are produced by our brain, and optical activity, and are affected by the condition of the light in the room. If we are sitting with our eyes closed, and the sun comes out, lighting the room, we experience the brightness. The moving shapes and changing brightness don't matter! We deal with them by gently returning our attention to the breath, at the breath-point, again.

INTRUSIVE THOUGHTS

Intrusive thoughts will also draw us away from the breath-point. In a few moments, we aren't meditating, we're following an attractive or worrying thought. We have to go back to the breath-point, leaving that intrusive train of thought. We let our awareness of the breath, at the breath-point, take all our attention. We do not have any feeling of defending the breath-point, a centre of peace, against stray thoughts, because the attraction of the breath-point is far greater than the competition from stray thoughts. It's like all exercise: the more we practise, the more effective we become, and the easier it gets. But even when we are experienced, stray thoughts intrude. Don't ever think that you have to finish your period of sitting without being troubled by thoughts. It is the ability to *return* to the breath-point which is the essence of the technique.

CONCENTRATION

We can't actually see the breath-point because our eyes are closed. As we try to focus our attention on the breath-point, we have a strange sense of seeing in the dark. We have to get to this point, the breath-point, and hold it with concentration – not with any tension in our body.

There is a gentleness in our concentration. The smaller and clearer the point of focus, the easier we will find it to pursue our concentration, and the less we will be bothered by stray thoughts or external sounds. Holding our concentration has to be achieved without strain. We will tend to have the sense that the peacefulness of the breath-point is more attractive than anything else. If we feel strain, we let the point go, and come back calmly to it again. We are conscious of the movement of breath at the breath-point; but we are not directing it.

We sometimes find that we can't focus closely on the breath-point. All we have is a broader area of attention, in the vicinity of that cool point where the breath first touches the nose. It doesn't matter. We use that broader focus the same way. We watch the rise and fall of the breath in that space. We are drawn to an area of peace, a space instead of a point, where there are no thoughts. If we are distracted by changing shapes, we gently return to the breath-point, or the broader focus of the breath.

On other days, we may find that our mind is still, and there are fewer moving shapes. We can get a much clearer focus on the breath-point, and hold it more easily. After we have been sitting for a while, our body will quieten down, including the breath. The breath may become only the faintest stirring, but always realised at the breath-point. However faint or uneven the breath, we don't try to control it.

ABOUT MANTRAS

Could one of these be a help in your task to stay on the breath-point?

A mantra is a solemn sound which is used in some forms of religious meditation to help concentration. It usually has a dignified sound like the tolling of a church bell. And like a church bell being tolled, it is repeated over and over, either in the imagination or out loud.

Before you say, *I think I could do with one of these*, we have to disentangle the religious or spiritual ceremonial from the exercise. If you're involved in some form of religious or mystical ceremony, a mantra may be appropriate, but it's irrelevant to personal meditation; it's another of those props I've said you don't need.

COUNTING

I have a practical suggestion. Counting – in the mind. I say counting because it has no spiritual, ethical or moral significance, and can be a mere aid to concentration without any mystical overtones.

Count *one* on the in-breath, then *one* on the out-breath, *two* on the in-breath, *two* on the out-breath, *three* on the in-breath, *three* on the out-breath, *four-four* and so on, up to about six. Don't go into double figures because the mind isn't supposed to be computing numbers.

Up to about six, the count gives continuity to our effort to stay on the breath-point without strain. We go back to one when we've finished the sequence, and begin again. It doesn't matter if we don't reach the same count every time. It doesn't matter if we fumble the count. And we don't need to try to remember how many sets of six we've done.

The counting exercise is also helpful when we are meditating under difficult conditions – we have pressing worries, or noise inter-ruptions. It gives a robustness to our prac-tice, without effort.

After we have been counting for a while, we will feel we are steady on the breath-point, and conscious of the movement of the breath. Then we can let the counting go, or it will naturally fall away. When our breath becomes very faint, and irregular, counting is less helpful. We can hear the hush of our own breath as it rises and falls; that sound in itself is solemn – the breath of life.

Remember, this is essential – a count, if you want to use one, is imagined. We are not moving our throat or lips. Counting is only a temporary assistance. When we settle down, the need for counting should disappear, but if you feel most comfortable when you count the whole session through, that's OK. Do what is easiest and most effective for you.

How do I know I'm actually meditating? We're meditating when we're focused on the breath-point, and our mind is clear, conscious only of the movement of the breath. I know it doesn't sound like a very big deal, but it is.

HOW LONG AND HOW OFTEN SHOULD I MEDITATE?

We should try to meditate every day, even if we can only spare a few minutes. It's good to make it a habit, like cleaning our teeth or jogging.

Fitting meditation into a busy life is a problem. Twenty minutes or half an hour in the morning is plenty but five minutes is beneficial. Before eating is best. If we can do it twice a day, that is, again in the evening, that is better. But these are ideals. Most of us can only manage once a day, and sometimes not even twenty minutes. But don't be put off if you have trouble finding the time. Any time given to personal meditation is helpful to us.

You'll probably find your evening session quite different from the morning one. Your mind will have been active in taking on all sorts of impressions during the day, and will be inclined to jump about much more with stray thoughts than it is in the morning. When the mind is fresh from sleep, personal meditation is certainly easier. But again, it's good practice, like jogging up a slope, to see if we can manage a session when the mind is tired or overactive.

HOW DO I KNOW HOW LONG I'VE BEEN SITTING? WILL I FORGET TIME AND MISS MY TRAIN?

Time tends to go fast in personal meditation,

particularly when you have acquired some experience. Half an hour's practice usually seems to have been a much shorter time than that. So it's quite sensible to use an alarm clock if you have one that doesn't make a ticking noise. That way you can put time out of your mind. Again, it doesn't matter if you don't have an alarm clock. I don't use one, and I seem to be able to guess about twenty minutes, and then I look at the clock, and try to guess another ten, usually coming out a few minutes either way of the ten.

When we do personal meditation we don't lose consciousness. Quite the reverse. We are in a peaceful state, but our mind is clear and sharp. All forms of meditation are in a sense the reverse of hypnosis, which involves a form of sleep. We'll hear sounds outside our meditation room, but we have to turn away from the thoughts these sounds give rise to. When we are really focused on the breath-point, external noise doesn't stir thought so readily. Obviously, the mind is such a complicated organ that our consciousness of time passing remains intact, but superficially "out of mind", if we are concentrating fully, until, like an alarm clock, the mind says to us that half an hour— or whatever time you had in mind – must have passed. You won't miss your train.

PHYSICAL EXERCISE FIRST?

Limbering up a little physically can help to tone us up before we settle down to personal meditation. It's not necessary at all, merely a good idea. If you have a regime of bathroom exercises, don't stop them. Meditate afterwards, before breakfast, when you're feeling sharply awake. I say before breakfast, because sometimes food in the stomach brings a dozy feeling, and we want to be sharp. But there's no rule about it. Meditating after food is infinitely better than no meditation.

I'm afraid jogging or any other strenuous exercise isn't useful at this point, unless you can take a shower, and have time to let your pulse return to normal.

I have in mind some simple stretching exercises for the arms, legs and trunk.

You should only do the exercises you feel comfortable with, if any. And of course you should not attempt them without medical advice if you have any physical problems. The exact number and nature of each exercise is something you should decide, depending on the time you have, and how you feel. Experiment a bit. End up with what makes you feel toned up.

One very important point. We should keep in mind that we are limbering up for meditation. It's best to close our eyes when we perform the exercises. We can feel the exercises gently pulling on our muscles. When we are doing them, we try not to think of anything else. We feel one set of muscles gently flexing, then another. We are trying to *become* those stretching muscles. This session is a kind of mini-meditation.

THINK WHEN YOU HAVE TAKEN UP YOUR POSTURE ...

Let's think what we are going to do before we do it. We are going to be *here*, and it is *now*. We are going to relax in our posture, close our eyes, and find the breath-point. We are going to stay centred on the breath-point, watching what our breath does ...

AM I GOING TO GET A SPECIAL BUZZ?

Yes you are, at least occasionally. It is a distinctly physical sense of well-being, generated by the feeling that we are doing something enjoyable, an enjoyment of the moment when our mind is clear, and at rest. Everything else seems far away, all the troubles, cares and noise.

But we don't expect this surge every time, and we don't get frustrated if we don't get it. The special feeling of well-being is a spin-off, not an objective, and our practice will be just as rewarding if we never get it. It's not something we can aim for. If it happens, great!

There will be times when personal meditation is difficult, even though we have been practising for a long period. We may have serious worries, or be feeling very emotional about events in our life. Clearing our mind, and calming down, will seem almost impossible. *But this is the time to practise.* We won't have a feeling of well-being on these difficult occasions. Trying to keep a clear mind may seem like a struggle. But we should try. After all, calm is what we need, and calm is what the practice can give us.

EVERYTHING IS GOOD
IN MEDITATION

As my Swedish teacher said, *Everytink iss gutt in meditation*. If we find we can't concentrate because we're so upset, it's right to keep trying. A few moments of concentration is better than none. We go back to counting. We may not get beyond three, but we try. We go back to one as many times as we need to. We find we gradually make an impression on those painful thoughts, gradually create a centre of calm. And when we finish our practice, a confidence that calm is within reach, will go with us.

If we are disturbed by anybody, or if an intrusive noise starts, or if we can't get comfortable, or our leg aches, we don't regard personal meditation as spoiled. Every tiny step adds to our beneficial experience. We simply start again when the interruption has gone, or go somewhere else. Remember, the essence of personal meditation is *return* to the breath-point.

Personal meditation during noise and inter-
ruptions, or in an uncomfortable place where
we can't sit down, or where it's wet or cold,
is still valuable practice. Try it. Often, we
find that we become distanced from the
interruptions or discomforts. They shrink to
the small inconveniences they really are,
while we remain calm and detached from
them. The interruptions and discomforts are
themselves only our thoughts, and like other
unhelpful thoughts they can be rejected, or
diminished to irrelevance.

THOUGHTS THAT DISTURB US

TAGGING OUR THOUGHTS

Leaving our intrusive thoughts and returning to the breath-point is where we get the
exercise, and develop our ability to concentrate. You could try this little trick – go
through a process of tagging the thoughts
that come to you, identifying what they are.

For example, *Worry about yesterday's interview*. Now leave the thought, with this tag attached, and return to the breath-point. Another thought comes. We identify what kind of thought it is. *Anxiety about my bank balance*. We leave it, and return ...

Most of the thoughts that arise will be on matters that we can't do anything about in the time that we're supposed to be meditating. We've set aside this time to practise. The world can manage quite well without us in this time. The idea of tagging the thought is to get it into proportion, to recognise that it's a concern that can be put aside, at least for the moment, and needn't intrude.

Once we get practised at tagging, it's a process which takes only a millisecond of our attention. Eventually, we are able to refine our ability to classify a thought and tag it with a word: anger, sorrow, noise, fear, nonsense, irrelevant, fanciful. All thoughts, for different reasons, can be discarded for

the moment. They needn't stop us meditating. This is our dedicated half hour or five
minutes. As we carry out this process of tagging thoughts, and returning to the breath-
point, we're moving closer and closer to a
calm, clear present. And when we move
from personal to Living Meditation, we carry
not only the sense of calm, but a deeper
understanding of the quality of our
thoughts.

HOW AM I DOING?

The other category of thoughts that will
come to you are those about how well the
meditation is going. These are insidious, in
the sense that if you are a learner, you need
to be conscious of what you're doing, but
meditation isn't thinking about the meditation process, or congratulating ourselves on
doing well. It's staying on the breath-point
with a clear mind.

Our thoughts may run like this when we've

been sitting for a few minutes: *I seem to be going well now. Great. I'm counting. I'm noticing the breath. Oops! I seem to have messed up the count. And now I've lost the breath-point. I'll pick up the count first* ... and so on. This is thinking about the process – quite understandable thoughts – but it's not meditation.

The best advice I can give is to rehearse the process quickly in your mind as you settle down, and then dismiss it. *Posture, right. Relax into the here and now. Find the breath-point. Stay on it* ... We are conscious of the movement of our breath. We prefer the peace of the breath-point to all thoughts – even those which comment on how well or badly we're doing! The temptation to think, I'm doing a great job, and I like this, is over-whelming at times, but we have to leave it and return to the breath-point.

JUST DO IT

There is a rule which will help you. *Just do it*. You will know this famous Zen saying, and what it means here, is that there is a point at which we have to stop thinking about how to meditate, or the good effects of doing it, and just get on with doing it.

The example often quoted is of a diver, on a high board above a pool. He has practised every aspect of his technique in the gym, and from the board. He understands precisely what he has to do. From the moment he steps on to the board to take his competitive dive, the time for thinking about how to do it has gone. He just has to dive.

So it is with personal meditation. Once we have set ourselves up, and eased into our practice, and we have the breath-point, we give it exclusive attention. We feel the superior attraction of peace, against the muddle of our thoughts.

❋ 2 ❋

THE UNREAL THINGS ABOUT REALITY

WHAT PERSONAL AND LIVING MEDITATION CAN DO FOR YOU

I have explained briefly what personal meditation can do for you, and how to do it, and now I want to look at why it achieves results. You can treat it as a stress relieving exercise, or as a first step in a view of how our lives work in practice.

The first is helpful, but limited, like a walk in the fresh air. The second leads to an enjoyable way of living. The more we understand about how the things that affect our lives work, the more likely we are to be able to enjoy.

WHY IS PERSONAL MEDITATION
A FIRST STEP?

Because the starting point for all our thoughts has to be us, each one of us, personally. It's our thoughts that are dealing with the problems of living. And it's very personal. People can tell us that such and such is true, but unless we experience the results, all the telling in the world isn't going to succeed. Personal meditation is an experience, not a doctrine. It's not a package of beliefs which you have to swallow. It has no religious, spiritual, moral or ethical rules or principles. How could it? It's an exercise, like push-ups. It is a way of quietening the mind, as the first step in being able to see what is happening to us. This is the basis to go on and deal with life most effectively.

BUT WHO SAYS THERE ARE PARTICULARLY
USEFUL THOUGHTS OUT THERE?

Nobody. There is no prophet. There is only you, and a process, and an age-old question,

which human beings are always asking:
"Who or what am I, and what's happening?"
The answer is to be *experienced* in Living
Meditation, and the attitude to life which it
creates – but I can tell you the simple and
pragmatic answers you will find: (1) that we
have many illusions about ourselves, (2) that
much of the time, human beings live in a state
of unsatisfactoriness ranging from mild discomfort, to pain, and (3) that everything,
including ourselves, is changing all the time.
You already know these things without meditating at all – but as we develop awareness
through Living Meditation, we see that these
three observations have crucial importance in
the process of life of which we are part – and
our ability to cope with it, and enjoy.

THINKING ABOUT WHAT YOU ARE THINKING

We often hear the phrase, *Everything is in
the mind*. It's one of those truths we know

quite well without really appreciating its significance. The fact is that we don't have any life outside what we think. If our mind stops working, we're dead. So what we think is crucial. Living Meditation encourages us to understand that we can think what we want to think – the useful thoughts – and put aside the rest.

THE MIND HAS A SURREAL COLLECTION OF THOUGHTS

The whole purpose of both personal and Living Meditation is to get a clearer take on life, and how we can cope most effectively and enjoy. What we observe about the mind – thinking about what we're thinking – is that it is a ragbag of thoughts. Some are years old, some are fantasy, many are based on instant passions like "She's very rude" or "I don't like this man." Our thoughts are often a catalogue of unfulfilled wishes or desires, "I want this" or "If only I had that." They well up and disappear suddenly. They aren't permanent. They aren't substantial. They're like puffs of smoke. Many are neither reliable nor believable.

To steady the mind and focus it upon a particular subject isn't as easy as it sounds. As we find in personal meditation, when we focus our attention, other thoughts often intrude uninvited, relevant and irrelevant. The natural state of the mind is one of constant movement. It is sometimes compared to a monkey. The monkey chatters and jumps about in the trees, falls into silence, and then begins to leap and chatter again. The mind is rather like that, quiet and dreamy for a moment, then nervously processing a huge variety of images. It can veer from gentle amusement to frantic anxiety in a matter of seconds. It provides an endless video show of images, which often have no great importance.

This is the nature of an ordinary, healthy mind, and we come to understand that these thoughts are not "reality" or "life," they are merely wandering thoughts, and they are permissive. If you indulge a line of thought, however unimportant, it can go on and on.

YOU CAN CHOOSE TO THINK DEPRESSING OR CHEERFUL THOUGHTS

We know that we live in the quality of our thoughts. Pleasant thoughts, pleasant time. Angry thoughts, miserable time. Anger and hate are painful for us. Calm and tolerance make the moment enjoyable, or at least give us a feeling of lightness. In Living Meditation – in daily life – we're sensitive to this divide in the flow of thoughts.

I have a way of describing this divide. I call the useful thoughts, those that contribute to calm and tolerance, the white path, or white thoughts. I call the useless ones, those that contribute to tension and pain, the gray path, or gray thoughts. I'm sure the distinction will be obvious to you. I don't use the words positive or negative, because a lot of our most unconstructive thoughts have a lot of drive behind them – like anger and lust – and in that sense are positive. Also, positive and negative don't cover a whole category of regrets, dreams and wishes, which might be positive or negative, but which can be unhelpful. White and gray seems clearer.

If I ask you whether you're on the white or the gray path right now, I think you'll know. Ask yourself many times in the course of the day, whether you're on the white path or the gray path. If you're on gray, you'll soon see the value of moving over.

We follow our own inner suggestions. If we feel, before we do something, *I'm going to hate this*, it's fairly certain we will. We'll suffer the discomfort we've anticipated. But if we say, before we've taken on a task we're not keen on, *I'm going to enjoy,* we'll usually find that we do, or at least find some aspects to enjoy.

Occasionally, an associate of mine has meetings with members of a committee, one of
whom he doesn't respect much. He told me
that when this member wasn't present, he
found the meetings pleasant; when he was, he
used to find them irritating. In fact, he was
thinking of leaving the committee. I said,
"Why don't you say to yourself, before a
meeting, that you're there because you believe
it's worthwhile, and you're not going to allow
anybody to spoil that." He said, a bit cynical-
ly, that he'd give it a try. Months later, when I
asked him how the experiment went, he said,
"I changed my mind-set and it worked. I
ceased to get impatient at this man's com-
ments. I just let his irritations arise and pass
away – and come out from the meetings with
much more constructive feelings. And I think
I'm more effective in the meetings."

We've cleared away the gray clouds in our
head, and replaced them, not precisely with
optimism, but with a critical awareness of
what we're thinking. It seems very obvious,

doesn't it? Many people confuse their own depressive thoughts with reality, blaming the external happening that they can't do anything about it – forgetting that they can do a lot in their attitude toward it. If we can get our attitude to events right, dealing with the problem is so much easier. Often, nothing can change what has happened outside us. The only factor that can lighten it for us is our attitude.

Personal meditation practice will make us more confidently the master of our thoughts. In Living Meditation, we should choose the useful, rather than drift along with the useless. The mind is like a storehouse. We can fill it with flowers, or leave the carcasses of dead chickens there.

LIVING IN THE PRESENT – THERE'S NOWHERE ELSE!

This is not a call to a reckless kind of living – live now, pay later. It is another obvious fact of life. We have no alternative. Life is a series of present moments.

THE PAST

We know that there is no actual past, only written, filmed and spoken memories of it. History is what the historian writes, but he cannot write everything that happened. And he cannot know, let alone record, all the different points of view on the event he is writing about. The past is a story, and it's a story which depends upon who is telling it. It isn't an actual reality, in which we can live, or to which we can return.

When we look back personally, it's the same. We look into a mist. We may think that we have the "real story" about a past event. But we can't know what the other people concerned were thinking, because their experience remains largely locked inside them, even if they were friends or relations of ours who shared the experience. Everybody has a slightly different view about a past event in which they were involved.

The Roberts family used to live near us. One of the sons, George, had a violent argument with his father, Mark, about the way the father was treating their sick mother, and as a result the son, who was about seventeen, left home and the pair sadly never spoke again. The daughter of the house lined up on her brother's side, and one of the other two sons supported their father. The remaining son was neutral. I knew George well, and we had many perplexing talks about how different members of the family could differ over a situation which they all asserted that they knew, and understood. But that's the way it is!

People frequently regret the past, as though it could be remodelled. It is not very helpful to say, *if only I had done this or that*. The actual past can never be revisited except in the imagination. It can make no sense to agonise about doing things we now feel we should or shouldn't have done; that is self-inflicted pain.

I used to have a manager in my office, a very efficient accounts clerk of about thirty, whose family circumstances changed suddenly, when he was at school, and his parents couldn't afford to send him to university, as they had his sisters. Hugh responded to the family demands on him to get a job, and missed his further education. I said to him more than once, "It's not too late to qualify in accountancy now. You'd do it easily, and it would mean a lot." "I should have done it years ago," he'd reply regretfully. He dwelt on how he might have acted differently – might have found a way to qualify, despite his family circumstances. Hugh could never entirely accept the consequences of how he had handled the past. He chose to live with the regret, instead of walking on.

There is no harm in reflecting on the past,

learning about it, and trying to learn from it, but when it comes to fantasising or regretting the past, in Living Meditation, we will be very conscious that time spent dwelling in the past is *time in which we don't live in the present.*

The past can spoil the present. Our regrets about the past tend to become fainter when we think in this way. We can accept the past because it has happened and it can't be reshaped. We'll be conscious that our regret isn't regret about something that exists now. The problem we have is with *our* thoughts. We're going to resist carrying any unpleasant emotional baggage relating to the past, because it's painful. We try to accept and become easy with our past. We forgive ourselves. One thing we can be utterly sure of, if we are tempted to regret the past, is that it isn't going to make a jot of difference to anybody but us, and eventually it's only common sense to lighten our self-imposed load. The past isn't life. *Life is now.*

THE FUTURE

Thinking about the future is one of the great sources of enjoyment of the human race. The future is full of hopes and dreams. And there can be nothing wrong with pleasurable anticipation, and planning, provided we remember it may not work out, at least in the way we thought it would.

A distant relation of mine had a haulage business which he sold at a huge profit while he was in his late sixties, and he settled down with his wife to enjoy the proceeds. His only son, Nick, went to a good school, but Nick could never quite make it either to a profession or a very highly paid job – although he tried everything. When Nick married, he and his wife Heather, lived with periodic handouts from his father to supplement his income. It's not an uncommon story, so far, is it? But you could tell, when you talked to Nick and Heather, that they had their lives on hold until Nick's father died. That was when they would inherit. Life was going to be different then. This is a sad story, because a couple of years before he died, Nick's father lost nearly everything in the stock market. Nick and Heather were finally, after a lot of agonising, resilient enough to adjust to relying upon themselves, but they had wasted quite a few years living in their desires. Living for tomorrow is not a good idea.

In Living Meditation we become aware that the more we dream about the future, and identify ourselves with it, the more unsatisfactory we may find the result, because we've become more closely wedded to those desires. And the more our thoughts are on the future, the more we deprive ourselves of our only living space – now. Having taken satisfaction from our plans, and the good things that we anticipate will happen tomorrow, we can put them aside as a pleasant *maybe*, and come back to the present.

THE NOW

In Living Meditation we are therefore aware of the depression, unhappiness and pain that can be caused by overlooking *now*, the moment in which we're really alive, and drifting off, instead, into reveries about the past and future. We realise that our enjoyment cannot be found in yearning for some other moment than the one we are actually living in *now*.

SLOWING DOWN TO APPRECIATE
THE MOMENT

Sometimes, living now is a matter of slowing down, and seeing what's in front of us. In the rush of the day, we're often too busy to see. I went to visit a business executive colleague in hospital, where he was taking some enforced leisure as a result of a heart scare – he was in his late forties. The doctors weren't sure what was wrong, and they wanted to observe Harold. He was the kind of person who never sits still, and does six things at once. Seeing him in his office, or even at home, I had found that it was hard to get his undivided attention. He was always on the phone, sometimes two phones, and his PC, and talking to somebody present at the same time, or reading papers, doing *big* things, like company mergers. Well, Harold was scared by the doctors, and he agreed to do just what they said. When I greeted him he was reading in bed. I noticed a paper flower on the side-table. After a while, I asked, "Who made the flower for you?" "I did," he replied, giving me an odd look. He was about the last person I would expect to take the time to do this. "You did that?" "Yeah, I went to a little therapy class, and you know, I had a good time. I learned how to make a flower. You never know, I might go into business, making paper flowers."

In Living Meditation we learn to value this moment, we pay attention to it, letting go of anxiety about other times. We become calmly interested. We observe what is happening. We may even make a paper flower.

ENJOYING THE MOMENT

*Y*ou may be thinking, *The day consists of a lot of boring things, getting up out of bed, dressing, thinking of the tasks I have to do, washing, suffering the journey to work, getting sweaty about making it on time, doing those things in my in-tray that I hate, all that. Even if I do take the rush of the day more slowly, how can I enjoy it?*

Enjoyment is a state of mind. If you eat your sandwich at lunchtime, and think of a difficult meeting you're going to have in the afternoon, you might as well be eating a Kleenex with mayonnaise. But, if you can say to yourself, *I'm going to take my time eating this ham and salad sandwich, which is a favourite of mine. I'm going to really taste it – and enjoy* – you will enjoy. Try it. Taste every mouthful.

Deciding that you're going to enjoy something quite ordinary and commonplace usually leads to real appreciation. A young woman I know works in a nursery. Rosemary once said to me, "You've got no idea how tense and fraught my day is. The kids are demanding, and their parents are twice as demanding. It's awful!" I said, "Wait a minute, this is your job, you trained for it. You have to decide you're going to like it, or get out." Rosemary asked how she could like it. I said, "Try *deciding* you're going to like it every day, as you go in the front door in the morning, complaining mothers and all." When I saw Rosemary a few months later, I asked her how the job was going. "It's coming along," she said. "Taking it quietly, and thinking in terms of the good things in it, has helped me a lot. I love the kids, you know." In Living Meditation, it's not merely thinking "nice" thoughts, it's a much more subtle appreciation of how we are governed by the quality of our thoughts, and the determination to get our thinking right.

You're getting ahead of me, because you're thinking, How can I be calmly interested in the present if it's awful? Now might be a domestic row, a car smash, or a war. True, the present might be horrible, but we have to face it anyway. Taking refuge in hopes and dreams, or plunging into depression about something in the past, won't cure the difficulty in the present. We do have to face some tough situations in the present, and I deal with the really big ones in the chapter on Acceptance.

TO SUM UP

Personal meditation makes us conscious of what we are thinking. Living Meditation makes us question whether our thoughts are useful. It makes us conscious of the divide between depressing thoughts (the gray path) and optimistic ones (the white path). We devote a lot of the present to regrets, dreams and wishes (which are often gray). We can't actually live in the past or the future. Whether we like it or not we have to live now. Living Meditation gives us the ability to focus on the moment, live in the moment effectively, and either enjoy it, or at least make the best of it.

THAT FEELING OF DISSATISFACTION

The reality of our lives is that most of us bumble on, nursing our regrets, and hoping that our wishes will be fulfilled, always looking over the fence to see whether there is something better there – and if there is, wanting that, and hoping for it. This is the way of living that I'm going to deal with here.

NOTHING IS QUITE RIGHT

Most people suffer every day, and certainly fairly often, from a sense of dissatisfaction. I mean everything from mild irritation, through annoyance, and anger, to outright physical pain. Nothing seems quite right, often for long periods of time. We aren't enjoying. We aren't smiling much. We're head down, dead set on all the things we've got to do. We feel pressure. Things seem to turn out disappointingly. Our relationship with our partner is, well, far from perfect; our job which we've worked so hard to get is not shaping up as we'd hoped; our son is at a very difficult stage; we can't afford that new house that we really need; a good friend has let us down; we're worried about our health; we're having difficulties coping with disablement; and so it goes on. It's unsatisfactory. And these problems, and dozens more like them, colour our thinking; they make it gray. This is putting aside all the more serious problems we can be confronted with in the present moment, like illness, permanent disablement and death of a loved one.

DO MONEY AND EDUCATION HELP?

Not necessarily. Sometimes they make it worse. The more money we have, the more options we have. Many seemingly attractive new avenues open up for us – friends, jobs, vacations. When we don't have it, at first thought, money seems the very thing we need to reduce our dissatisfaction. But expectations rise with incomes. A first class passenger on a plane can be as bitterly disappointed about the service as an economy passenger. He or she expects what they regard as first class service, and nothing less will do.

Two people at my work took a luxury flight to New York to celebrate their marriage anniversary. This was great. The airline arrangements were perfect, and the staff made a fuss of them. But when they arrived at their Manhattan hotel, they found it wasn't the upmarket place they had anticipated. In Eric's words, "It was a dump. The travel agent screwed up in spades!" He was furious. Eric and Chloe spent their first night in the room they hated, and then a day of misery in long distance telephone arguments with the agent about changing hotels. "It cast a shadow over us," Chloe told me. "We decided not to change hotels in the end, because we were only in New York for three nights, and moving would have meant another day of disruption. We decided to endure it." I wondered myself whether the accommodation was so bad it had to spoil the vacation, but there was a strange irony yet to come. New York had a blackout, a power failure which lasted over twenty four hours. Eric and Chloe found themselves in the fortunate position of being only twelve floors above the street, while those who were fifty floors up at the Sheraton and the Hilton couldn't reach their rooms and had to sleep in the downstairs lounges and passages. Eric and Chloe had (in their minds) lost one game, but by sheer chance won another.

Obsessed with the belief that life can, or should, be "better", people with more money often have a sense of entitlement. *I want it all, and I want it now*, in the words of the Queen lyric. It's a painful yearning.

I do some work for a drugs charity, and one

of our residential patients, Don, was a pleasant and well-educated twenty-five year old, from a prosperous home. He'd been indulged by his father with cars – which he promptly smashed – and then he'd taken to drinking and finally to heroin – and he had been hooked. When I spoke to him, he said, "I guess I wanted everything. I just wanted to keep that buzz going." Don had found out the hard way that you can't keep that buzz of pure pleasure going. Of course, he's an extreme case of *wanting*.

In the search for satisfaction, the now, when we're alive and capable of enjoying, passes by, neglected in a haze of regret and desire. Some dreams can be pleasant, and in Living Meditation we will enjoy them no less, but we will be focused on the present.

LIVING IN DESIRES

We can see that a cause of dissatisfaction –

put in its simplest form – is that people live in their desires. This is the ego delusion; that sense of wanting and being entitled to everything. As sane, healthy human beings, we recognise that our desires are unlimited, and can never be fulfilled. Events move too fast, and our desires are too fanciful, excessive and changeable. It is simply impossible to retain what is pleasant in our lives, and get rid of the unpleasant. We know this. We experience it, and see others experience it, every day.

The Joplins are a young married couple I know, with a good relationship, healthy kids, a steady income and an everlasting problem, and discomfort – about houses. In their search for perfection, nothing seems right. I'm aware of four houses they have had, and the present one doesn't suit them. First, it was the size, then when they pulled out the stops and bought a big place, it was the neighbourhood. You had to have security, and you couldn't be easy about walking the streets nearby in the dark. When they moved again, Lisa complained about the neighbours. Now they are settled in a new area, and the problem is distant traffic noise. They'll probably be on the move again soon. The perfect house probably doesn't exist, but how long will it take the Joplins to find out?

THE ILLUSION OF PERMANENCE

Let's take a look at the way we think as a cause of dissatisfaction. We like to think in terms of permanence, stability and predictability. We "set ourselves up" in our lifestyle, thinking of the home, the family, our friends in the community, and all the services which support this way of life, like medical care, education, and security as ongoing and permanent. Day in, day out, we expect this to continue in the way we understand. We live highly organised lives, set train times, set car routes to the children's school or our work place, meetings and social events scheduled. We want to know what is going to happen next, if there are going to be changes. And, we have a strong sense that we are controlling events.

In Living Meditation we see this picture as an illusion which leads to disappointment. Permanence, stability and predictability are wishes, not realities. And the disappointment arises from the fact that they don't always happen, or go on happening.

In Living Meditation, focusing on a changing present, we will see life as anything but predictable. Changes may happen quickly, or slowly, but they are always happening. Everything, from the watertight roof of the house to the quality of the teachers at the school, changes. Children grow up and leave home; relationships break down; parents die. The uncertainty of life makes it extraordinary. When we focus closely on the changing present, it's like having 20/20 vision for the first time. Everything looks different, and life is by turns wonderful – and chaotic.

The reason our attention is on this ever-present movement, this *process* of change, is that we know that we have our eye on the ball. Change is the ball. We have to adapt and meet it. It's no use yearning for the way things were yesterday, before our friends moved away, when we had a pleasant boss, when there was a good hardware store in the high street, when the water service was twenty per cent cheaper, and there were six more trains on the line. It's all change. All the time. In Living Meditation, we are conscious that failure to adapt means irritation, anger, grief.

We are aware that the way things are depends on our personal perspective, and there can be many different perspectives. Our youthful views will have been more free, while an adult viewpoint is often worked out over years, and probably shared with others of the same class or culture. After a few years of being programmed as an adult, the *Been there, seen it, done it* mentality takes over. The answer is more or less automatic.

DISOWNING EXPERIENCE AND TRYING A FRESH VIEW

How do we take a fresh view in Living Meditation? Only by disowning a lot of experience, trying to see events freshly, and accepting that there are a lot of different views. That's difficult to do, because our responses are often automatic as a result of having been through that situation before. Or because other friends, or members of the same community, have dealt with the situation in a certain way and we feel we ought to follow.

In Living Meditation we pause and think, what is really happening here? If we can do this with an awareness of the extent to which we have been programmed by our culture and our community, it's easier.

PROGRAMMED THINKING

Obviously, a lot of rules and routines make life easier. The price we pay is that like trained dogs, we react in certain ways to certain situations. Friends of mine, the Coleman family, who live in a small town, decided to give their daughter a very elaborate wedding. When I spoke to Joe Coleman about it, he said, "You can't get away from it, that's what's expected around here." The Colemans felt that their "position" locally required them to have a big celebration, hiring the local hotel and having Champagne on the green. They couldn't really afford it, but they just couldn't take what they viewed as a loss of face in the neighbourhood. The Colemans were pressured into acting typically, like the way they thought the family next door would act, when perhaps a different approach was required.

The pressures of our class and culture are only the more obvious signs of being programmed. The way we use language, and the effect of books, newspapers, films and television, all cause us to think along certain lines. In Living Meditation, we want to free ourselves, as far as possible, from unthinking responses that have been absorbed unconsciously over the years, or at least be aware of them. It does not mean that we will unnecessarily oppose our community, or our employer, or our friends, or become an eccentric in our views. It simply means that we are wary of programmed thinking and automatic responses. We will try to see events from both, or many sides.

SUMMARY

A sense of dissatisfaction dogs us. Money and education don't help all that much because we live in desires, and they tend to expand with income. Experience tells us we can't exclude all the unpleasant things from our lives, and live on a permanent high. We realise that programmed thinking may lead us into trouble, and we want to try to make a fresh response to problems.

The big question, of course, is how Living Meditation combats dissatisfaction.

❋ 3 ❋

UGH! WE HAVE TO FACE LIFE AS IT IS

I've mentioned the *dissatisfaction* that often afflicts us, and now I want to mention the other two observations (part of the crucial trio which I listed before), the significance of *change*, and our illusions about the *self*. Both of these, because they are in conflict, are causes of our dissatisfaction. In order to deal with our lives we need to understand the effects of change, and the effects of our illusions about the self. In Living Meditation we are using the awareness which is refreshed by our personal meditation to focus on the immense significance of these effects. It's not just a matter of saying, *Sure I understand about change and the ego-delusion, so don't go on about it!* These two factors are present, conflicting, in some

79

shape or other, in all our problems, and are an ever-present part of our meditative consciousness. The ego wants certainty, and life isn't certain.

EVERYTHING IS CHANGING – AND ALL THE TIME

We live at the point where change is happening – now. We are well aware of the cycle of birth, growth, decay and death which is shared by all living things. And science has made us aware of the process of change in seemingly solid matter throughout the universe – all those energy particles buzzing around. Just as there is a cycle of life for all living creatures, so all seemingly "dead" matter – stone and iron – degrades and changes. We see apparent solidity and permanence around us, but in fact, everything is changing, including ourselves. The now is the result of a very complicated chain of action and reaction to change. Nothing is still.

CHANGE LEADS TO UNCERTAINTY

We have a fair idea what will happen in the course of our daily routine. We get the weather report. We have a bus timetable. We expect electricity at the throw of a switch, and water in the tap. Our day looks fairly settled, but events we cannot know about are always contributing to make the present moment slightly, or perhaps surprisingly, different. No matter how hard we try to keep things as they are, we can't. Sometimes the weather report is wrong. Relations don't arrive when they say they will. The paint on the kitchen wall suddenly looks shabby; the dog gets sick; a row develops at work; we twist our ankle. Our lives often look ordered and predictable, but they aren't. The unexpected happens, an earthquake, a drenching storm, a heated argument, a sudden accident or illness. Nothing is certain.

EXPECT THE UNEXPECTED

This fact that we can't divine the future is a

key point of focus for us in Living Meditation. We accept how uncertain and chaotic life can be. We expect change. We expect the unexpected. We are that much cooler about it, whether it's a big event, or a tiny deviation from our known and loved routine. It's all the easier, because we can never fully explain or understand why events happen as they do.

There is a saying that if a leaf falls in a Brazilian jungle, an avalanche will eventually cascade down a Swiss mountainside. Perhaps untrue, but a colourful reminder of the complexity and mystery of why things happen. Often there's nobody or no one distinct person to blame. And we're aware that even if there is, we usually can't control either events or other people. So we don't lose sleep over it. This understanding is crucial to living in the present moment and enjoying it.

But what about us? We're the ones who have to deal with this uncertain situation.

WHO ARE WE?

We need to know what or who we are, if we are going to face the present. We often hear people say "I need time to find myself" or "I need to work out who I am." These and similar phrases are used on the assumption that there is a "self," a "you" or a "me," which is fixed. The only problem is to find the self! Our ego has come to be regarded not merely as an aspect of our feelings, but an identifiable thing, attached to us, almost an organ like our heart or lungs. We talk about "his ego" or "my ego," and some people believe there is a self which is more or less constant, and that they can find it.

MOVING THE SELF OUT OF THE WAY

One reason why it's refreshing to clear the mind in personal meditation is that it moves the self out of the way. For once we are not in the picture. The mind has come to rest at the breath-point. So many of our thoughts are about what *we* want, what *we* are going to get, what *we* think about what happened yesterday, how *we* react to a friend's problem, or how *we* are concerned with relationships around us. Our view of ourselves is almost always in the picture. Some of these thoughts are happy, like anticipation of the company of friends, or sexual daydreams, but a lot are discomforting and create an underlying tension because they are based on unfulfilled desires, imagined hurts, or guilt about our inadequacies.

THE ILLUSION ABOUT "OUR" POSSESSIONS

Soon after birth an infant begins to distinguish between "self and "other." In the small world of a child there is a self to be protected, and an other to be guarded against. The sense of self defines itself in relation to possessions and externals: *my toys, my mother, my dinner*. And this definition goes on as the child becomes an adult: *my coat, my house, my business, my rights*. Sometimes we are tempted to think of ourselves as the sum of these possessions or attributes, but as we recognise when we think about it, the truth is, they are not us. We may own and appear to control things but they are not us. We may get a lot of pleasure from them, but that does not make them into us. In Living Meditation, we see that we are not our possessions, any more than we are our behaviour, capabilities or beliefs. These attributes may give a changing definition of us, but we have not actually found ourselves.

THE DIFFERENT SELF OF YESTERDAY

The self is different today than it was yesterday – only a little perhaps, but different. Day by day we look different. We learned something yesterday, so we react differently today. The self of today is markedly more different from the self of last week, and much different than the self of five years ago in ideas, experience and appearance. My local newsagent recently had a burglary at his

TEACHING YOURSELF TRANQUILLITY

shop. The thieves stole a lot of goods, and made a terrible mess. I called in the other day. "How is it, now?" I asked, noticing the cleanup. "Oh, OK," he said, trying to be cheerful. "You know me, always the same!" But he wasn't the same. He couldn't hide his bad experience.

We're driven to the conclusion that we're us on the day we present ourselves. We're ourselves only in the present moment, different yesterday, and tomorrow.

DO OTHER PEOPLE REALLY KNOW US?

If we can't find ourselves in the list of possessions or achievements we call *mine*, or in the different selves we manifest over the years, the views of others are equally unhelpful.

Have you ever been to an "encounter group," where people who know you, tell you candidly what they think of you? It can be quite surprising, because people are showing you a side of yourself you never thought about. I worked in a company which started encounter groups for senior executives. After the first one, I remember talking to Michael, who had a high reputation as a finance man. "I was shocked," he said, and he shook his head in disbelief. He was a quiet, very logical person, never known to be ruffled. "What happened?" I asked. "They, well most of them, said I was a bit cold, uncaring. They didn't use the word, but they meant ruthless." Michael didn't think he was ruthless, or particularly cold, but that was the way he looked to others. His kids probably saw him as a warm, affectionate daddy.

If we try to assess ourselves honestly in the eyes of those about us, the different views will become apparent. A brother will see us in one light, a husband in another, an employer in yet a third. Each close personal friend we have will see us differently, because we will tend to relate differently to each, and perhaps share different activities with each. We may be loved for our kindness by one person, and criticised for our meanness by another. Which is the real you or me?

Clearly, none of these personal views of us, taken by other people, is correct in being complete and permanent. We show a different self to whoever we are addressing. We can see that the permanent self is an illusion. We are what we think we are today. But we might change our mind tomorrow. And we are also what other people think we are. And they might change their minds, too. There is no precisely definable you or me – only a personality in constant change.

TAKE IT EASY AND FORGET ABOUT YOUR IDENTITY

In Living Meditation then, seeking to relax into the present, we are not worried by trying to find our "real" selves. We don't have to search for our identity because it is pointless. It doesn't mean that we are any less self confident

about our capabilities. Indeed, this understanding of the haziness of the personality is
inclined to make us more confident in our
dealings with others, because we see that
same effect in other people. Having thought
about this, we don't have any sense of loss in
being unable to find our bright, shining ego.
We know it's an illusion. And we're aware of
the problems other people have trying to
maintain theirs. *We are lightened by the
knowledge that the self is an unclear, changing concept.* When we have to take some stick
from other people, we don't register it as a
dent in our ego, and dealing with life
becomes that much simpler.

WE ARE UNIQUE, AND ALIVE!

The personality may be elusive, but *we each
own our experience of being alive now*,
exclusively. Nobody can share our experience without being inside our skin. We are
separate, like billions of candles blowing in
the wind. *We share the experience of being*

alive now, and the urge to remain alive now.
In Living Meditation we recognise that this is
probably the most important phenomenon
that human beings can conceive. Literally,
everything else we can know, and experience,
is – must be – subordinate. Without the experience of being alive now, and the will to live
now, there is obviously no life.

This important piece of knowledge assists us
in Living Meditation to focus on the present
moment because it is uniquely *our* moment.

A fellow meditator told me this story: As a
boy he lived quietly and reasonably peaceful-
ly with his mother and father who seemed
attached, if not openly affectionate. When
the father died, after a long illness, Geoff and
his mother were by the bed. His mother's
shocking comment was, "Thirty wasted
years!" Geoff told me he could never forget
that, because he hadn't the slightest idea that
his mother, whom he thought he knew well,
felt that way.

We may have lived with our partner or parent for a long time. We may know a lot about them. We may empathise with them very sensitively, but we can never know precisely what they feel – and what they have felt in all their experiences when we weren't around. There will always be shadows of the unknown between people. It's one of the great mysteries of life, and the reason we never lose our thirst for stories, in fact or fiction, about other people.

The slenderness of our knowledge of other people becomes more obvious very quickly, as we move from family and close friends to work colleagues, neighbours, acquaintances, then on to other people in our community, and to people who don't share our culture or ethnic background. When we get to animals, it's quite impossible to imagine what it's like to be them, although a few fiction writers have made fortunes trying. What is it like to be a shark or a giraffe?

THE UNIQUE IMPORTANCE
OF THE MOMENT FOR EACH OF US

So we're all separate. The problem of really knowing what it is like to be somebody else, or an animal, can be touched by art, but probably never solved by science, and its significance for us in Living Meditation, thinking how to live in the present, is to emphasise our separateness from each other, our uniqueness. It's not just another boring day, or a day the same as yesterday. We are *each* unique beings, and the most important thing we can be sure of is that we are alive at this moment. It's our unique moment. Our heart is beating. We can feel the breath rising and falling in our chest. And hopefully we can see, smell, touch and hear, but if we can only experience some of these senses, we still have the feeling of being alive. It's a sensation we share with others, and want to preserve above all others. Too often, we take it for granted. We're more worried by our bank account than we are gratified by being able to

92

walk, and talk, and feel, and taste this unique moment of our experience.

THE RELATIVITY OF HAPPINESS

To those of us who are well, there is one experience of life, and to those of us whose life is threatened, or are disabled, there is another. A man of thirty-five in my street had a serious car crash and spent days on a life-support machine. Colin was a hustling businessman and a great networker on various associations and groups. He was a good partner, but he didn't have much time for home. When I saw him after the accident, Colin had been discharged from hospital and was sitting in his garden. "How about all your commitments?" I asked. "Never mind them," he said, "I'm taking one day at a time." It's a common enough phrase. Have you noticed how a person who has had a near-death incident, perhaps injury in a car crash, perhaps cancer, revalues their life? This revaluation nearly always takes the form of pausing, of looking at what is happening around them, of concentrating on the moment.

In Living Meditation we take every day, one at a time, but the near-death person has sometimes had to have the understanding that the moment is precious, forced upon him or her. The sheer beauty and importance of being alive *now* has made them grateful for the modest present moment that they now have.

THE SMALLER WORLD
OF THE DISABLED PERSON

People whose mental and physical capabilities are deteriorating as a result of disease or trauma come to inhabit smaller, more limited worlds, but still experience their unique sense of being alive now. You'll have seen how their reduced world is as valuable and important to them as the larger world of the person in good health, and that is why many sick people are resigned to their illness, and capable of showing enjoyment.

Bill and Clara were a couple in their thirties. He was in robust health, wanting to indulge in his sport of walking, and Clara had a serious mental disease which eventually confined her to residential care. Bill used to visit regularly, and he said to me, "I couldn't bear to live like that. I'd rather be dead, than be in a bed or wheelchair all my life." And he meant it. But Clara wasn't making those comparisons. She had adjusted her horizons, and was quite capable of enjoying the small pleasures of a day in a residential home. Enjoyment is relative. Enjoyment is what we – each of us in our own unique way – think it is.

In Living Meditation, we are focused on the fact that our will to live, although shared with others, is unique to the world of our mind, whether it is the glamorous life of a film star, or the strange reality of a sufferer from Alzheimer's disease. We can see that one life is not measurable against another. They are merely different. So we have this understanding of the unique value of the present moment for ourselves – and for others.

SUMMARY

We and our lives are changing all the time, which raises the perennial problem of how to cope with constant change, and the disappointment it often brings. And second, we tend to live with the illusion that life ought to treat us in a certain way because we are whom we think we are. This is a source of disappointment, because our egocentric expectations are often defeated. Our personalities are elusive, and changing, and while we share the will to live with all other humans, we experience life, each of us, in our own unique way. The present moment is unique for each of us, and therefore uniquely precious.

❈ 4 ❈

ACCEPTANCE OF THINGS
AS THEY ARE

ACCEPTANCE IS ABOUT LIGHTENING
OUR LOAD OF TROUBLES

Acceptance of things as they are is not difficult to understand, but not so easy to apply in everyday life. Acceptance means giving a calm reception to situations we mightn't like; it means living in harmony with our environment, chaotic though it may be. When we're initially angry and frustrated by events around us, it's not easy to take the line that we're not really frustrated or angry at all. Living Meditation helps to keep the importance of acceptance in our mind, and makes it easier; it gives us a different slant on these anger-producing moments. We're less likely to become angry in the first place. And the further we can go, in everything that happens, toward real acceptance, the lighter our load of troubles, and therefore the happier we will be.

WHY ACCEPTANCE HAS TO BE WHOLEHEARTED

If we're merely playacting, pretending to accept, while actually harbouring all the feelings of anger and irritation, we haven't moved an inch along the way. The whole point of the kind of acceptance we want to practise is to relieve our anger, to free our thoughts, to lighten the moment, not to conceal our true feelings. Concealed ill feeling can be as painful as overt ill feeling.

ACCEPTANCE EVERY DAY

Acceptance isn't just for big issues. It is needed at the level of the ordinary day's events, like dragging ourselves out of bed, getting the children's breakfast, waiting for the bus, haggling at a work meeting, shoving into the crowd around the bar to get a beer, and so on. Every moment is a valuable moment of our lives, and Living Meditation puts it in focus. It may be an OK day really, but we have all sorts of frustrations and aggravations, from running out of tooth-paste, to having a hard time with our boss at work or seeing the doctor. And some of the happenings can be quite serious when it comes to the rights and wrongs of relation-ships with our friends and neighbours.

ACCEPTANCE MEANS FIRST A CALM ACKNOWLEDGMENT OF THE PROBLEM

Personal meditation feeds through into Living Meditation, giving us a calm and even-handed approach to events. Effectively we are meditating when we hit the problem. Instead of reacting with instant anger or irri-tation, we are asking what has happened, and measuring the extent of our ego involvement.

This may happen in microseconds or, if the problem is more complex, in a longer time. There is the problem, and our reaction to it. In the humdrum little frustrations of the day, it's often a matter of simply understanding that this is the way things are.

Acceptance doesn't mean that we have to approve things we disapprove, or not be offended by acts we feel are offensive. In the first instance, it merely means that we have to acknowledge that the problem, separate from "us," exists.

ACCEPT THAT LIFE IS MESSY

These happenings are going to make us tense, irritated, a little depressed, and spoil our day – if we let them. We understand that events happen in strange and difficult ways, and people don't behave as we'd like them to. The unpredictable. That's the way it is. That's our point, this understanding that life can be messy.

DON'T MAKE YOURSELF PART
OF THE PROBLEM

Our next point is the realisation that what we're dealing with here is our thoughts. We are dealing with our reaction to events, not the events themselves. The events have happened – our computer has a virus, we've sprained a wrist, the plumber hasn't answered our urgent call and the bathwater is coming through the kitchen ceiling. We *have* to face these facts, and we're not going to make ourselves part of the problem: that is, we're not going to make the situation worse by taking on a burden of miserable thoughts, bad temper, anger and frustration. What's the point? It won't do any good.

So we're calm at this point, and the question is, what do we think and do, and why?

THE SPLIT BETWEEN HELPFUL AND
UNHELPFUL THOUGHTS

Let's deal first with our thoughts. Our

attention here will be on the split between helpful thoughts, *helpful to us,* and unhelpful thoughts, *unhelpful to us.* And the split is simple. On one side, we have a range of self-ish and anti-other people thoughts – hate, anger, greed, blame, ill will, malice and many more of this kind. These thoughts are like poison, and they poison us. This is the gray path. On the other side, we have calm, good-will, kindness and friendly thoughts, the white path. We all know, instantly, in any situation, which side of the divide our thoughts are forming on.

UNHELPFUL THOUGHTS CAUSE US PAIN

Which side to choose? We know that if our thoughts are on the selfish, anti-people side, there is a price to pay: everything from dis-comfort to pain. That is why they are unhelpful. I met one of the people in my office, going in the entrance recently, and he had a nasty scowl. "What's the matter, Graham?" I asked him. "Is the sky going to fall in?" He spat out his reply. "Some bastard cut me up on the M1 this morning, a suicidal lunatic in a big, fat Mercedes! I'm so bloody furious!" It was going to spoil his day. He'd be talking about it at morning coffee, and no doubt to his wife that night.

In Living Meditation our reaction, on the instant, might be the same as Graham's, because these feelings are instinctive, but we would quickly realise that the incident was over, and our day wasn't going to be upset by an anonymous driver. Graham was driving a small Ford, and he had personalised the driver of a *big, fat Mercedes* as aggressive and greedy. In Living Meditation we tend to avoid personalising issues if we can, because there's really no other person there; instead, we attribute the happening to what it is – the random forces that operate in a complex society. The reality is that Graham didn't know the driver of the car, but because he visualised the driver, he had somebody to fix his rage upon. Every day you could say we're buffeted around by various forces, natural and human. There's no need to take it further.

Thoughts of hatred, anger, greed and envy might seem at first to be natural, and even justified by the situation we are in, and there can seem to be a kind of brutal satisfaction in them, but there is still pain. Such thoughts fill our head like a black cloud. They blot out the sunshine of the moment. I know the extreme case of a woman whose daughter was horribly murdered, and she has fought over years to keep the killer in prison. The price of her personal pursuit of "justice" has been agony; it is etched in deep lines on her face, and you can feel it in her voice and manner. The priest who tried to give her some ease said to me, "The killer destroyed two people." Violent and angry thoughts aren't something we can permit ourselves because it's "justified" by what has happened to us. These thoughts are like a disease, toxins in the blood, and we don't willingly submit to disease.

THE EFFECT OF CALM OR KIND THOUGHTS

We also know that the thoughts on the other side of the split, tolerant and kindly ones, don't hurt us – the white thoughts. On the contrary, they ease the way. In many cases, if a very bad event has happened, we can put it out of mind more easily. We're not wrestling with our own ill feeling. We're not tortured by it. We don't drag it with us like a dead albatross. We accept and move on.

WE DON'T ACCEPT BECAUSE WE'RE SAINTLY

We're not high-minded in accepting the way things are. We don't do it because it's morally "right" or because somebody has said that as decent people we "ought" to accept. We're not hot on forgiveness because we're "good". We accept because it makes our life easier; it lightens our load. Our decision to calmly accept what we can't do anything about anyway, or to be forgiving in attitude if there's a particular person to be

blamed, is made out of enlightened self interest, but of course the other people involved
get the benefit of our calm or kindly attitude.

THE SPLIT BETWEEN HELPFUL AND UNHELPFUL ACTIONS

What about our actions? We know that violent thoughts poison our mind. What about
violent actions? We know that violent reactions to something nasty that has happened
only tend to get people's backs up. As soon as
we start using violent words and actions, people defend themselves by responding in the
same way. Then we have to answer their violence. Punch and counter-punch. The gray
path and the white path obviously apply just
as much to actions as they do to thoughts.

VIOLENCE BEGETS VIOLENCE

Two neighbours in our street are locked in a
terrible battle. It started when Roger Butler

lost his temper as a result of the Foster's barking dog. Maybe the dog was annoying. Butler shouted over the fence, at the top of his voice, "If you don't shut that f*****g mongrel up, I'll cut it's throat!" The Fosters retaliated by waiting until Butler had guests sitting out in his garden enjoying the afternoon sun, and started up their incredibly noisy lawnmower. Butler's guests had to flee indoors. Butler called the local noise prevention unit, and officers arrived at the Foster's house, but with no result. The Fosters waited a few days and chopped down a delightful tree in their garden which happened to attractively shade part of Butler's property. I believe Butler has now threatened court proceedings. So it goes on. Folly and pain for two families. All from a few angrily spoken words.

We know that violence can, and often does, escalate in a tit-for-tat game. Whole communities and nations can be caught in the circle. We see it every day on TV, political killers who claim that their murderous acts are merely a just reprisal for what their adversaries did to them.

PEACEFUL RESPONSES TEND TO BE MET WITH PEACE

On the other hand, the experience of most of us is that a calm or kindly reaction to a situation we don't like often, if not always, leads to a peaceful response from the other person. We've all seen examples of this. When I was travelling on the underground recently, a soldier objected to being pushed by another passenger. "Get off me!" the soldier shouted, and shoved the other man, who was big and tough looking. "What the hell do you mean?" the big man roared, and grabbed the soldier. The scene was set for a fight. Then the soldier relented, saw he had been hasty. "Ok, ok," he said, "I'm sorry. I thought you crowded me." A few words of explanation and the pair agreed it was all a mistake in the crowded carriage.

When we're confronted with something or

somebody that makes us angry, we are conscious that we can encourage events to move either along a violent, or a peaceful path (gray or white) depending on our reaction. Acceptance of the hundred and one hiccups that occur in our lives every day involves having tolerant and kindly thoughts and actions – and the reward we get is that in our reaction, we avoid the irritation and anxiety that others have to face.

COPING WITH THE LOSS OF SOMEBODY DEAR TO US

I'm sure you're thinking that there are some events which are so bad that acceptance, as I have explained it, isn't possible. One of these events might be the loss of a person you love. Everyone who suffers the death of a person close to them, suffers shock. It takes time to understand what has happened, and the more so if the death has occurred in violent or unusual circumstances. And it can be made very much worse if we are conscious that our friend or relative suffered before he or she died. We empathise with that pain. We can imagine what it must have been like. It's no use pretending that there are any nostrums to take away our immediate pain. Shock and grief are perfectly natural.

But very soon in Living Meditation, we will start to think about the reality of the situation. The loved person is dead and cannot be brought back. The sad event is in the past. What is left is our sense of loss, our consciousness of a space left unfilled, our pain. We will question how long this ego-load of our problem is to be carried.

BEING SORRY FOR YOURSELF

We would hardly be human unless we showed respect for the dead, and were deeply affected. But in time, and it will be a different time for different people, in Living Meditation, we will come to understand that we are the real object of grief. We are mourning for ourselves. We are sorry for ourselves.

A very close friend of mine lost his wife very suddenly with a brain tumour. They were basically a happy couple, but had been having a few matrimonial troubles in the months before Eileen died. I sat with Brian in the park, more than eighteen months after Eileen's death, and he talked about her. "I'm plagued," he said, "by the knowledge that I didn't make things easy for her towards the end. I just can't forget it." "Are you thinking about her, or yourself?" I asked. Brian started to say that of course he was thinking of Eileen, then his honesty took over. "I guess I feel guilty." I asked him if there was any need to go on and on, regretting the mistakes he had made, and spoiling his life. "It's almost masochistic," I said.

We will see the sense of relieving ourselves of the weight of grief or guilt, because beyond a point, there is no reason to carry it; it does nobody else any good, and it does us a lot of

harm by blighting our life in the present
moment. This isn't inconsistent with contin-
uing to remember the deceased person with
love, provided the memories don't lapse into
the pain of feeling sore about our position,
and feeling sorry for ourselves.

BUT SUPPOSE THE LOSS HAS BEEN CAUSED BY SOMEBODY?

Here, we may understandably have instant
feelings of animosity toward the person or
group we blame for our friend or partner's
death. This is an additional layer of pain, particularly if it is necessary for the killers to be
brought to justice. Some people never recov-
er from their depression, and hatred, and lust
for vengeance in such a case. They seem to be
pushed on to the gray path permanently.

PERSONALISING HATRED

In Living Meditation we realise that even in this

extreme event, we have to lighten the burden on ourselves. We try to view the wrongdoer not merely as an evil person whom we think ought to suffer for his wrongs, but as an unruly force over which we and our dead friend had no control. If our daughter was killed by an avalanche while skiing, or by falling from a horse when riding, we wouldn't get angry with the avalanche or the horse. We'd accept that it was a force of nature. In the same way, in Living Meditation, we try to avoid personalising hate and anger. An evil person who has harmed our friend is, in essence, an evil force. Focusing our hate upon him is quite pointless, and only hurts us.

We know that we are all subject to a maelstrom of forces, human and natural, in which some of us are hurt, or swept away. The world is a very risky place. In Living Meditation we try to see personal tragedy in this more detached, impersonal light. And we don't do this because it's "the right thing," or because we're trying to show we're a good person. We do it because we know we'll feel better, we'll be free of a horrible burden. What has happened is bad enough, without having to carry the burden of it in our thoughts indefinitely.

CARRYING THE BURDEN OF ANGER

*Y*ou can see what I mean when I say that acceptance is not an easy attitude to have, and especially when death or injury or illness affects our loved ones, or when illness or disablement results for us. But you can also see that, in the end, it all comes down to our willingness to carry a pointless burden of grief or anger. In Living Meditation, we will struggle to free ourselves from that burden, however sad and hurtful our loss.

And at the same time, we have to beware of a much more trivial, but corrosive, problem.

GENEROSITY OF SPIRIT

There is an element of acceptance here. I expect that when I said kindness tends to be returned with kindness, you thought, *Maybe so, in general, but so often small kindnesses aren't noticed, and aren't returned at all.* And that, unfortunately, is true. How do you handle these situations? Suppose you've written a very sympathetic letter to somebody in trouble, and they haven't responded. Or you've given a friend a sum of money when she left her purse at home, and she's forgotten to return it. Or you've taken a couple to dinner, and paid the bill, and they've never returned the favour. You may have carried out a dozen small acts of generosity like this in the course of a month.

In Living Meditation we try to couple our act of generosity with generosity of spirit. In other words, the act is done without thought of recompense. It's not done with an unspoken condition that we expect the favour to be returned. And the reason for this, again, although it's on a very small scale in our life, is that we don't want the burden of the unpaid debt. We don't want to think that an acquaintance, whom we might meet at our club, owes us a few drinks and never buys one. It's a cloud over the relationship. We don't want to think whenever we see a person in the street, "She never did thank me for helping her."

In Living Meditation we cultivate a generosity of spirit when we are dealing with other people. I was once the attorney looking after the affairs of a very disabled person. Over a period of years, Kay received notes from a woman friend, who at one time had been her best friend. The notes from Moira always said more or less the same thing – "I can't understand why you don't get in touch." The couple had parted over some difference that as far as I was concerned was lost in the clouds of the past. Whenever I asked Kay to write back to Moira, she always refused.

Finally, Kay's condition deteriorated, and she could no longer speak or think clearly. Then another "I don't understand" letter, virtually the same, arrived from Moira. This time, Kay couldn't have answered if she wanted, and I felt I had to reply. I told Moira that it was too late for explanations, or a meeting, because Kay was too disabled. I said I thought it was sad that Moira had only been prepared to go as far as writing a letter asking a question, when she might have made a visit. And that it was equally sad that Kay could never bring herself to respond to Moira. Here were two people who weren't prepared to take the trivial step necessary to bridge the small gap between them. It was a balance sheet friendship.

We don't want to be running any of our relationships on a balance sheet basis – *if she does this, I'll do that* – it casts a pall over our enjoyment of the moment. If we behave like this, we can't enjoy, because we're always referring to our balance sheet, and finding out that the other person owes us something. It's another example of self-imposed misery. If we seriously think we ought to be paid back, we ought to candidly ask for repayment. If we sincerely don't care about repayment, it gives a marvellous freedom of thought and action, an opens the possibility for enjoyment.

ATTACHMENT

Attachment to material things and people, especially family, isn't generally considered to be a fault, but it's linked to fear and worry about losing something or someone. Genuine acceptance often involves overcoming our attachments. Whether it's attachment to a person, *my friend, my son, my wife*, or a piece of property, *my car, my farm, my house,* the attachment is based on the protection of our ego. These people and these pieces of property we consider to be "ours." We don't intend to lose them, and if we did it would be painful. The attachment itself hurts, because there's always the possibility we might lose, and of course if we do suffer loss, it hurts even more.

A couple who are distant relations of my wife have an only child, a daughter. Sarah was an attractive and clever girl who got on famously with her parents, Neil and Vera, but when she went to university, she decided that instead of coming home in the vacation, she would move into an apartment with her girlfriends. Neil and Vera were stunned. Neil went to the apartment, and there were unpleasant scenes when he tried to persuade Sarah to come home. He used all sorts of arguments about Sarah's age, her financial ability, her safety, but the heart of it was that Neil and Vera wanted "their" daughter with them. Sarah never did return, and a couple of years later, this still rankled with the parents; they were uneasy and hurt. They couldn't give up their attachment. Parents are quite naturally attached to their children, but they

TEACHING YOURSELF TRANQUILLITY

have to give it up.

Attachment to property can sometimes be extreme. A scratch on your Ferrari can spoil your day. An elderly widower with whom I served on the same charity board was looking rather ill, and I asked him what was troubling him. He said, "I'm completely preoccupied with getting this money of mine over to my kids." I knew Tom was well off, and spent his days managing his investments. This was very trying for him, and so was getting around the death duty laws. "Why don't you hand over your work to an agent, and go on a big holiday?" I asked. He looked at me completely askance. "I could never do that until I've worked out how to get my assets over to my family." Tom was virtually roped to his property and the worry of it was affecting his health.

In Living Meditation, we are conscious that attachment to other people, and material things, brings anxiety. There's nothing wrong with having friends and family and property, and we enjoy all this, but we understand that nothing is "ours." We don't own or have the right to control other people (except our young children), however closely related they may be. We may be so lucky as to be blessed with good relationships, and material goods, but we realise that our connection with them is our good fortune in a changing world, not our absolute right. And if the unpredictable forces of change intervene to change our personal relationships, and perhaps reduce our material goods, we don't get hung up about having lost something of "ours." We accept what has happened. We're quick to appreciate that if we don't sever our attachment and accept, we suffer. We're able to go on our way with a lighter heart.

ATTACHMENT TO HABITS AND VIEWS

We also realise that attachment can relate to a whole lot of our habits and practices, everything from attachment to a particular pudding to attachment to a political view. Our consciousness of attachment, in all its forms, is helpful to us, because we can often look at an upsetting or depressing event, and say to ourselves, *I'm attached here. I'm tied to this person or practice or belief by a cord that hurts. What I have to do is to untie the cord, recognise change, accept it, and move on.*

GIVING

The opposite of being attached is giving. This is a helpful state of mind, and we try to think in the way of giving rather than being attached. It's so much more pleasure to give, and move along in life without all the prickly and painful snags of attachment.

There are various different kinds of giving. Giving way in some of our views and opinions gives us a different attitude to events, which might be the right one. It's always worth consideration.

Giving something you don't want

If we give something we don't want, like sending a sack of old clothes and books, which we were going to throw out anyway, to the charity jumble sale, obviously we aren't attached to them. It doesn't involve much feeling at all for us, although it's a useful thing to do.

Sharing something

If we share something we have, we need to watch how much we keep because that's attachment to what is "ours" or what "we" need. This doesn't mean that we should give rather than share; it means we're conscious of attachment – and if there's any strain about the sharing, we see it in a different light. We may be easy about giving a bit more.

Giving everything

If we give everything, or much more than we keep, clearly there's no attachment. We're free! It's a great feeling, never mind the good it might do to somebody else.

SUMMARY

Instead of approaching disappointing situations with anger, in Living Meditation we give them a calm reception, and accept that something beyond our control has happened. Angry thoughts are to be avoided because they cause pain, and angry actions are usually met with anger or lack of cooperation. In Living Meditation we cultivate generosity rather than operate balance-sheet relationships, and are conscious that attachment to people or property often reflects our unhelpful fear and worry about loss.

❀ 5 ❀
PRACTICAL TIPS FOR ENJOYING THE PRESENT

A SAYING FOR THE DAY

It's corny, but have a saying for the day, and make sure you repeat it to yourself often. You'll be surprised at how well it works. The saying puts you in the right frame of mind. You can have one saying, and use it all the time, or many, and change them day by day for variety – and for a slightly different angle on your thinking. If your feelings are unaccountably low, you're going to feel a whole lot better if you say to yourself, *I only have this moment, and I'm going to enjoy it!*

If we're not enjoying the present moment, we're reminded why immediately. We may

be having an irritating discussion with somebody we don't like, or we're worried about
being held up in traffic. We'll know instantly
that to lessen our own discomfort we have to
show a little tolerance or lighten up. The saying is a simple trigger that makes us remember that enjoying life depends on what we're
thinking.

Here are some sample sayings, but you can
easily make up your own:

- I'm going to enjoy today
- I'm alive now
- I'm going to think about what I'm
  thinking
- This is the first day of the rest of my life
- There is only this moment
- Am I thinking helpful thoughts?
- Am I on the gray path or the white path?

THE MOMENT OF CHOICE

There are a lot of these in the course of a

day, and we have to try to recognise them. It's the moment when something happens that makes us irritated, angry, envious, selfish, or just plain mean. It's a gray moment. Our spirits go down. Somebody or something is getting at us, and we're not going to have it. We react inside, if not outwardly. We are certainly not enjoying the moment, and, for the first second or two, we think it's not our fault. It's not us, it's *them*.

In Living Meditation we become used to recognising this moment immediately. We have developed and renewed the necessary awareness through personal meditation. It's a moment of choice. Are we going to choose pain – the toxin of anger spreading in our blood – or calm and understanding? This situation happens over and over in the course of a day, and we develop the habit of recognising the moment of choice, and refusing to take on the grief each time. It's life. Let's move on.

SEE THE PROBLEM AS AN OUTSIDER

When we hit a problem, it's sometimes effective to try to step outside the immediate situation. We back off, instead of lunging in with our irritation rising, saying what's on the tip of our tongue. Words seem cheap, and we may think we have the right to speak our mind, but if we use critical or hurtful or abusive words – on the gray, unhelpful side of the scale – we know they will cause pain to the hearer, and *to us*. Our temperature has gone up. We're getting hot. Our words are likely to escalate the problem, causing an additional layer of pain, because the hearer may lash back. We would be ratcheting up the dispute, not resolving it.

A colleague was having some building work done at his house recently. He was anxious to get it done quickly because of the noise and disruption. The builder's men were a day and a half late, and when they came, Dick gave them hell. As a result, they declined to start, and Dick had a dispute on his hands, and the serious inconvenience of not getting the work done. "I screwed up," he told me. "It wasn't until Anne [his wife] said to me that it was more important to get the work done, that I got it in proportion. It was too late then. I should have shut my mouth instead of shooting it off." Dick's wife was looking at the trouble as an outsider might have seen it. What Anne and Dick wanted above all, despite the delay, was to get the job finished and put it behind them.

How would an outsider, perhaps an onlooker, an ordinary person not involved in an event, see it? What would their attitude be to this unpleasant problem? If we try to look through their eyes, we may get an entirely different slant. We may see things that were not so readily visible from our own personal position. There's usually more than one point of view on these problems, isn't there? If we do this, we don't seem to be so much part of the problem, as part of the solution.

And we often get our targeting wrong when we're annoyed, don't we? Shooting from the hip at the wrong guy. Sure, there are plenty of people that cause us aggravation, and we can identify them. But a lot of our problems are not caused by the person we're abusing. The guard didn't make the train late – no point in giving him a piece of our mind. Chewing up the parking lot attendant isn't going to change the parking regulations. So often it's rules, company procedures, government offices, and all sorts of organisations that we get hot about, and we end up wanting to take it out on one of their people – who couldn't help it anyway.

I was waiting in the queue in the bank recently, and a woman was shouting at the clerk because her new credit card hadn't arrived. This was nothing to do with the clerk, although the woman didn't seem to realise it. The clerk sat calmly, taking the verbal abuse. You could see the abuse wasn't hitting the clerk. It was flying past his ear.

The complaining customer was red with fury. It was pointless, and painful for her. Don't let anyone tell you that you have a "right" to be angry. Just judge the result after you've blown a fuse. You feel terrible – as though a bulldozer had run over you.

In Living Meditation, we have a space of peace and calm around us from moment to moment. We want to protect this zone. When you're practised in Living Meditation, you'll look at the problem as an outsider might see it.

PUT YOURSELF IN THE OTHER PERSON'S PLACE

All the practical points I am making here are old hat, and maybe you already use some of them yourself, without any reference to meditation – but Living Meditation makes them specially relevant. How would you behave, if you were the *other* person?

In a lot of cases, this is helpful, because we

can immediately see that we ought not to get upset, but accept what has happened. We would have acted in the same way ourselves. We don't have a problem with our inner calm in this case.

A friend of mine recently went out of her house leaving a decorator painting a room. When she came back, she found the decorator had made himself a cup of coffee, in her kitchen, using her coffee and equipment without permission, and left a couple of cigarette buts in a saucer. She was irritated. 'What a nerve!' she said to me. "And I told him!" I replied, "Well, if you'd been working all afternoon with a paintbrush, and the owner wasn't there, wouldn't you have liked to make yourself a cup of coffee, and maybe have a smoke if that was your habit?" She reluctantly admitted she would. I wondered how much heart the decorator put into the work after that reprimand. These little snags that we get a dozen times a day are hardly worth thinking about.

Of course, the difficulty about putting yourself in the other person's shoes, is when we
are convinced that the other person has done
something we would never do. It could be
something quite small, like slowing us down
on the highway by driving slowly in front of
our car, or pushing into an airline queue
ahead of us. We are convinced that we would
never do these things ourselves. This makes
us all the more angry. Putting ourselves in
the other driver's place, or the queue-
jumper's place, isn't going to work for us –
but we better be sure, before we pass this
point up, that we'd never do what he or she
did. Not even if we were looking for an
intersection in a strange town? Or desperately anxious to get that last plane?

TRY TO SEE THE OTHER PERSON'S VIEWPOINT

This can work in a lot of cases, because
although you wouldn't necessarily act in the
same way as the person troubling you, you

can see how the other person's viewpoint on the event makes him or her act that way. Understanding of the event has a soothing influence. In Living Meditation, our awareness leads quickly to this understanding.

I was watching a football game on TV with a friend recently when he had an unsolicited phone call from a salesman, at an exciting point in the match. Harry answered the phone, but he didn't want any double-glazing or a new kitchen unit. He cut off the call rudely, and stormed back to the TV set, fuming, "Bloody cold-callers ruining my viewing. I missed that goal!" I said, "He's only trying to earn a living, Harry." After the game, when we were having a beer, Harry said, "You were right about that call. Some poor bastard in a call centre."

Of course, you might strike a problem where you can't sympathise with the other person's situation; for example, he's a criminal, or opposed to you politically, or he's somebody who's hurt a friend of yours. You have no respect for him. It's very difficult for you to be sympathetic. How do you deal with such a person?

We know that we can't set the clock back and reassemble the situation in a different way. The factor in the situation that we *can* change is ourselves, our thoughts and reactions. We have to get these on the helpful side of the divide, otherwise we will be the one to suffer – our rage, our frustration, our feelings of loathing and despair. We have the choice – abandon ourselves to self-imposed pain, or accept what has happened. In Living Meditation, we have found the answer. We will accept, and act with calm, compassion, kindness, understanding, whatever white path feelings are appropriate, and *we will feel light and free*. This kind of approach doesn't necessarily imply personal agreement or weakness. It's merely acceptance of reality, of things and people as they are. Our freedom is that we can deal with the event, without burdening ourselves with anxiety and pain. This really works. Eighty percent of our problems are trivial and not worth worrying ourselves about anyway, because we can't do anything about them. The other twenty percent are at least lightened by our calm.

GET THE MOMENT IN PROPORTION WITH AN OVERVIEW

You may find it useful to bring yourself back to the moment, and become conscious of your thoughts, and their relative importance in the scheme of things, by thinking of something bigger than yourself. Make a comparison between your problem and life itself. You might visualise yourself in relation to the billions of people on the earth, or as a speck in relation to the stars. How big does the problem of your overdraft look now? Or you might think of the achievements and qualities of a great person, living or dead, whom you admire. Compare yourself and your present problem with that great person. How would Gandhi or Abraham Lincoln deal with your argument with the man next door about his overhanging tree? When we do this, we're inclined to look quite modest and small – and we are. And so is the moment of difficulty we're having. Sit quietly. Relax. Listen. Smell and taste the now. Gently decline the load of unhelpful feelings. Meet the situation with calm.

WALKING AND EATING MEDITATION

Here are two mini-meditations which you can practice in the course of a busy day. The effect is to bring you back to enjoyment of the moment.

At times, we all do a number of things at once, don't we, our thoughts falling over each other? When we walk, we may also talk to a friend, take a call on the mobile, and look at the view. We're not concentrating on any of these things. Our attention and therefore our awareness is fractured. When we eat, we sometimes read a book, watch the TV in the kitchen, and talk to the children, all at once. We're bumbling along with all these tasks at the same time. Multi-tasking is good, and necessary at times, but it can turn our thoughts into a jumble. Here, the idea, if you have the opportunity, and have to walk a block alone for an appointment, or happen to sit alone in a café for coffee and a bagel on the way to work, is to use the moment consciously for Living Meditation.

When we're walking alone, we try to think only of walking. We feel the movement, from our feet touching the ground, up through our thighs and hips, to our upper body, our slightly swaying shoulders, and arms. We centre our mind on different parts of our body as we move, observing the feeling – in our arms, our hips, our thighs, our legs and ankles. We count our steps, in our mind only, up to about four or six – we get the rhythm of movement. Our mind is centred on our movement, other thoughts we ignore, and it they come, we switch back to consciousness of some part of the walking movement. It's very refreshing.

When we're eating alone, we simply eat, slowly. We taste and smell the food as we chew each mouthful, and drink. We keep our mind on the food and the act of chewing and swallowing, putting other thoughts aside. It gives a feeling of pleasure, and the food tastes better! We're consciously *living* this moment.

RELAX AND TRY A FEW MOMENTS OF PERSONAL MEDITATION

Try to practise relaxation during the course of the day, if you get a spare moment while you wait for a plane, or you happen to be early for a meeting with friends, even if you have to stand up because there's no seat. You don't need to close your eyes, but look at a point on the ground in front of you, find the breath, and bring your mind to the breath-point, easing other thoughts away, and creating a space of peace and calm. See if you can hold that position for a few moments. When you look up you'll feel here, and now, and that this is the moment. It's good to be alive.

SHARING WITH FRIENDS

If you have the opportunity to share meditation sessions with friends, this is good. It doesn't matter if others use a different technique. When a number of people meditate together there is a special sort of atmosphere which enhances the practice. I can't explain why, because I don't know. No more, I think, than a sense of shared objectives – calm and peace. Most of the time, we meditate on our own, but the opportunity of being with others ought not to be missed. Many towns now have meditation centres, and even airports. Whether you have the same meditation training or experience as others is of no importance at all. We all simply meditate in our own way. Even in a group, it is a very private experience for each individual.

The fact that in Living Meditation we don't get into the business of what is "right" thinking and what is "wrong" thinking, or persuade others that we're on a spiritual quest, doesn't matter. In Living Meditation, when we face a problem *in the street*, we deal with it with enlightened self interest – the most enjoyable or least painful way for us. This different way of dealing with our problems in life needn't affect our fellowship in personal meditation, with those who have a quasi-religious or mystical approach.

✻ 6 ✻
ANSWERS TO YOUR QUESTIONS

WILL MEDITATION AFFECT MY HEALTH?

Personal and Living Meditation bring enjoyment of life, and people who enjoy life are not usually thinking about being sick. Meditation is an exercise – and moderate exercise is good for us. If we have personal calm, and we can handle our life, even if it's difficult, we are bound to feel good. How we feel has a lot to do with good health, physical as well as mental. If we feel better, we probably are better.

Personal meditation need not tax us physically as an exercise; we just have to find our own personal way of dealing with the posture. If you have a disability that prevents you sitting in the ways I have described, find a posture with the least strain that suits you. The important thing is not precisely how you sit. The important thing is to practise.

The forms of meditation that I have described here won't have any adverse effect on the mental health of a normal person – quite the reverse – but if you think you have mental health problems, you should take advice before beginning. Some forms of meditation are not only used by psychiatrists and psychotherapists, but offered in books and courses as a way to improve mental health and, in particular, negative and depressive states of mind.

This book, on the contrary, is not intended as a medical tract. It's not about treatment. It's about enhancing our life, attaining tranquillity. It's for the ordinary person in good mental health. My argument is that personal and Living Meditation create the conditions of enjoyment which support a healthy mind and body.

WILL THIS AFFECT MY RELIGIOUS BELIEFS?

The short answer is "No". Personal and Living Meditation will enable you first to enjoy life, and in that enjoyment to interact with other people with tolerance and kindness. I doubt that this conflicts with any religion. The practice, as I have described it here, is a mental exercise. It is rooted in the here and now. It has no spiritual content. It has nothing to do with religion or with mysticism. It's true that the ideas that follow from awareness are answers to the age-old questions, *Who am I, and what am I, and what is happening?* But they are the pragmatic answers, about the universality of change, the unsatisfactoriness of human life, and the illusory nature of the self.

Religion deals with something quite different: the existence of God, and the spiritual destiny of human beings. Meditation in a variety of forms is a practice that occurs *within* Christianity, Judaism and other religions, and is a fundamental part of Buddhism, but in these cases it is linked to spiritual doctrines, and there is a special religious significance, as in prayers, of following the prescribed rictual or practice. There is no particular rule or rictual to the practice I have described. All we do is find the breath-point, concentrate on it, and clear the mind. The awareness of the moment which is created as a result has no spiritual content. We carry that through into our daily life. It's a case of being aware of the universality of change (a fact of life) and our ego-illusions (a psychological observation about human beings), and acting in a way most helpful or least painful to ourselves.

Personal and Living Meditation aren't dependent on any particular belief about how or why we came to be on earth, or what our spiritual purpose my be. All the background that I've described in the book – for example, about change, the cycle of birth, growth, decay and death, and the rather complicated reasons why things happen to us in the present moment, is based on what we all know from our experience of life. Three thousand years ago, when Buddha observed that the most significant thing about life was constant change, he didn't know anything about the movements of electrons and protons. He simply used the evidence of his senses. His experience told him life involves constant change. Our experience tells us the same. We don't have to be gurus or scientists. It's our understanding of the present in which we live that is important, not theories. The present isn't the firm, clear, predictable place we'd like it to be. It's uncertain and sometimes chaotic. Once we have adjusted our vision to this, life becomes easier to cope with.

We don't need any religion to tell us that our desires, which are limitless, are not going to be fulfilled, and that now, on earth (putting aside what might happen to our souls, if we have them, afterwards), we need to find a way to live with enjoyment. The way of personal and Living Meditation is to accept the uncertain present calmly, and to decline to shoulder the dark and painful emotions of anger and hate. What our practice does is show us *how* to turn, in each moment, from pain, to enjoyable and constructive thoughts and actions, and that can't affect any religious belief.

It is true that a lot of teachers of meditation in the West have extracted the practice from Eastern religion, particularly Buddhism, *together with* spiritual and moral precepts which are really part of the religion. The result is a mixture of meditation practice with predetermined moral, ethical and spiritual "principles." This is fine for those that want it, but I am quite clear that an exercise in concentration cannot in itself project spiritual, moral or ethical principles. An exercise is just an exercise. And I say that without in any way denigrating the "principles" in themselves. Indeed, a practitioner of personal and Living Meditation will be just as kind and compassionate to others as any other meditator, but he or she arrives there by a different route, the route of enlightened self interest.

IS THIS LIKELY TO ENHANCE MY CAPABILITIES?

If we have a calm, steady mind, and we are a light, friendly, tolerant and compassionate kind of person, we're likely to be liked and to be able to use our skills more effectively. It's a better launch pad for our talents, isn't it, than surliness, irritation and unfriendliness? If we accept others, they're likely to accept us, and that's the secret of getting on in life.

We can hinder our capabilities by being a grim, unpleasing kind of person whether at work, at home, at our sports club, college or interest group. We suffer both ways. We feel lousy about what we're doing, and other people soon get the message, and they return

149

it in kind. We don't forget that there's a downward spiral of all unhelpful emotions. Just as violence tends to beget violence in return, so irritation begets irritation in other people. Our relations with people are not going to improve if we're like this. It doesn't matter whether we're a mail clerk, or the CEO of the company, we can influence our personal relations, and nobody ever had personal relations that were too good. For our capabilities to thrive, we can't do without good personal relations.

Personal and Living Meditation quite naturally places us in a position where it's not an *effort* to be a little kinder, it's not a sort of special game we play to get a dividend. Being kinder, more genial, more friendly – it's real, a normal part of our enjoyment of life. And of course, it has the payoff that it usually gets the same reaction in those whom we deal with.

We aren't fooled that pretending to be

friendly is the same thing as being friendly. Pretending to feelings we don't have, just to get a certain reaction, is pointless, because we still suffer the pain of the situation. It's at the heart of our belief that we have to feel good, we have to enjoy – and then the right reaction comes naturally from others.

DOES LIVING IN THE NOW MEAN LIVING IT UP?

If you think living in the present moment means a frenetic attempt to cram every feeling and every experience into now, you've got it wrong. We don't have to dance all night, or eat a gargantuan meal as though it's our last, or make love until we're exhausted. Living in the present means accepting and enjoying every present moment as it comes. Life is simply a series of such moments.

What we are doing at the moment may be exciting – we're learning to ski – or fairly low key – we're walking in the park. Whatever it is, we have to accept it for what it is, make sure we're *there*, and not regretting something that happened yesterday, or worrying about whether tomorrow will be all right.

We are trying to be aware of the moment itself. What's happening around us? When we stop and ask this question we see all sorts of things we haven't noticed before. Life takes on a more interesting aspect. And how is what is happening affecting our feelings? Are the thoughts coming to us on the enjoyable side of the scale, or the depressing side? White or gray? If the thoughts are irritating and depressing, we try to understand why. We can identify how our ego is unhelpfully involved in these thoughts. We push away the unhelpful ones, and encourage those that take us on to the white path.

If we're doing something exciting like learning to fly, we won't have too much trouble in centring on the event, but many, perhaps most of the things we do permit the mind to wander, and like the complicated mechanism it is we can be running two or three trains of thought at once. The effect of this, usually, is that we're only half *there*, in the present moment. Our experience of the now is a blur, a confusion of the present, past and future. This leads to that feeling of unsatisfactoriness. We haven't resolved the problem we were talking about with a friend, and at the same time, we haven't tasted our dinner. But we've been trying to do both. We haven't been alive to the moment.

If we're normally operating like this, with our mind like a multi-channel video, the effect is vague depression. In personal and Living Meditation we settle calmly into the moment, dismissing the things we can't deal with now.

HOW DO I FIND THE TIME?

*Y*es, it's difficult, but look at what's on offer: calm enjoyment of life. We're all aware that we have to get some balance in our life between all the things we do. We don't have any trouble allocating time for exercise of the body. Surely, exercise of the mind is just as important?

The mind is the master, and the body is the servant. The body does what the mind tells it to do. It doesn't matter how fit and active a servant is, if the master is weak and depressed, the result is going to be poor. A weak and depressed mind can't do much with even the strongest body. This doesn't hold good the other way round – if the mind is calm, and clear thinking, it can probably make do with a less active body. The importance of understanding that the mind controls all, and that we can think the thoughts we want to think, is clear. We need the *time and practice* to make the mind a wise and clear-thinking master.

The actual time, twenty minutes to half an hour a day, plus the few minutes arising at odd times, that we allow ourselves to relax meditatively, and center on the moment, needs to be put in context. Our time will also be divided between work, watching sport, time spent in the bathroom, eating, socialising with friends, reading books and watching TV. When you think of the important and pleasant results we can achieve, meditation time isn't a big investment.

What about the case of a person who hardly has a waking moment that is peaceful? A working mother with a young baby, and perhaps other children, is an example. A person who has a long journey to work in the morning, has to rise early and gets home late, is another example. Yes, it's very difficult for them. I can make two suggestions. Try to find that peaceful moment when the children have, at last, gone off to sleep, tired as you are, or when you come home from work. As I have said, the end of the day, or when you're tired, isn't the best time for meditation, but it's certainly better than not meditating. And trying to meditate under difficult circumstances, like jogging uphill, is very good exercise. If you've experienced the practice under difficult conditions, when you do get a tranquil moment, you'll probably find your ability much enhanced.

My other suggestion is to try to combine these sessions with little moments of personal meditation during the course of the day. There will be a few minutes here and there, when you are alone, and it is quiet. You can close your eyes, settle on the breath, finding the breath-point, and feel that space of calm that is there for you. It's a good feeling. Five minutes, a minute, a half a minute.

Time doesn't matter at all that much, but we need to dedicate the time, whatever it is. We need to say to ourselves, *I have five minutes and I'm going to give it to personal meditation. Nothing else, just meditation.* We are actually setting aside these moments for our practice. If we consciously give up the period of time, it's much easier to deal with the rest of our thoughts. What we are in effect saying to others is, *You have to wait because I'm going to meditate, and I'll deal with you later.*

If you get into the habit of doing this mini-meditation quite frequently during the course of the day, during the odd moment, you'll find it rewarding in renewing your calm.

HOW LONG DOES THIS GO ON?

Forever. If we take up personal and Living Meditation, we won't want to stop any more than we're going to stop cleaning our teeth or taking a walk. It will be as important to us as our daily physical exercise, and probably continue longer. This doesn't mean that it's addictive! But the payoff is so great that we will find we don't want to do without it. The practice will become part of our routine, and we'll miss the lift it gives us if we're prevented from practising for any reason.

There are likely to be times in practice when we experience that special feeling of exhilaration in being at peace. And just as important as the time we specifically set aside for personal meditation is the effect afterwards. The calm feeling that we can direct our thoughts to what is really happening in the present, practicing Living Meditation, and away from the diversions of worries and desires.

The advantage that we will not want to give up is the ability to have genuinely tolerant and kind attitudes toward others. It's good for us, and for them. And it does a lot for our popularity. This is the basis of real enjoyment of life in the present, and there's no point in passing up the opportunity to be happy.

SHOULD I BE THINKING OF MY ENJOYMENT?

*Y*es, very much so. The person who is kind to others because he or she believes it is a virtue, or the right thing to do, is really following a religion or other spiritual belief. In personal and Living Meditation, we deal first with ourselves. If we have achieved calm and mindfulness, we can project tolerance and kindness toward others. We have become kind people in ourselves. Kindness is not simply a virtue we apply to somebody else. We'll be thinking differently about situations which would previously have put us in a rage, or depressed us. People will get the benefit, from us, of feelings and actions which are helpful to them.

Our enjoyment arises from our ability to cope with the difficulties of life with an easy calm. Without that ease about the way things are, we couldn't project kindness and tolerance. So the process starts with us. We develop the ability to identify what is happening, and adopt a state of mind which is helpful *first*, to ourselves, and then, because we've done this, it is expressed in our actions, and projected to others. *Our enjoyment of life is number one.* We can't be truly friendly if we don't feel friendly.

WHAT DO I TELL THE FAMILY?

Hopefully, they will understand that a lot of people do different things in this wacky world, and they'll at least know that meditation has a big following among people in all sorts of places. If we have to say something, it's probably best to say we're doing something that makes us feel better. And when we visibly become a little lighter about life, and start to enjoy it more and cope with issues more effectively, our family will be pleased. They get a benefit too!

It may not be much help to the family to try to argue the merits of personal or Living Meditation. It's not a pill. You can't say, "Try this." It's a process, a very subjective and personal process. They'll observe the result, and you can suggest that they have a look at the practice. In order to start, you've got to want to do it, and understand why you're doing it – you have to know and value the results you're going to get. It's not like making a wish, or declaring that you "believe" in something. *It takes time and practice.*

❋ 7 ❋
THE COMMON SENSE BACKGROUND

This is the section you can skip, unless you're interested in the ideas behind personal and Living Meditation.

As I hope the book shows, it's all about us personally, our attitudes, our behaviour and in the end, our enjoyment. We realise that if we get our attitude right, we project helpful feelings and actions toward others. There isn't anything in the book about being calm and kind towards other people because kindness is virtuous or morally commendable. The first and essential reason to be whole-heartedly kind and compassionate toward others is that it makes life easier and more pleasant for us. We are the starting point. Others get the benefit too.

I've summarised below the common sense points which the book covers, and I hope you feel that they reflect your own experience. They're the background. They are things we know. They're not rules. They're not about religion or mysticism, or medicine. They're not "ethical" or "moral" in themselves, though they do have ethical and moral effects. They're just plain common sense, or common knowledge, what we know mostly happens in life.

Personal meditation is the tool which makes us conscious, every day, of the importance of these points, and Living Meditation enables us to make use of them.

1. We want to live, even when we are disabled or dying.
2. And we tend to respect the right of others to live. Being alive is the wonder of our existence.
3. We are shaped by our upbringing. *This can widen our viewpoint – other people*

164

are differently shaped, and other people's ideas are important too.

4. We each have our own unique personal view of what we call reality. *Each one of us is on his or her own.*

5. We are seen differently by different people in different situations, rather than being solid, permanent personalities. *We have illusions about who we are.*

6. We, and the community we live in, are constantly changing. *There is no way but to accept the inexorable flow.*

7. The past doesn't exist except as selected memories of past events. *We can't live there.*

8. We can't predict the future. *We can't live there, either.*

9. We have to live in the present. *We need to continually make ourselves aware of the present moment.*

10. We become dissatisfied with life (ranging from mild discomfort to deep suffering), because what we want often doesn't

happen. *These defeated desires arise from our ego illusions and attachments to what we think are "ours".*

11. We either have to suffer that feeling of dissatisfaction, or accept the things we can't change. *It's a clear choice that we face a dozen times a day.*

12. Acceptance of things and people as they are in the present, involves not just showing tolerance, but being wholeheartedly tolerant. *Real acceptance is tough, but the more we succeed in having it, the easier we are.*

13. Anger related feelings are a personal burden which cause us anxiety and unhappiness. *Why take on this burden?*

14. We know that animosity and violence tend to evoke a similar reaction from other people, and peaceful behaviour tends to produce a peaceful reaction. *Confronted by the inexorable effects of change, we always have a choice, animosity or peace.*

CONCLUSIONS ABOUT LIFE AS IT REALLY IS

People sometimes say, "What do you mean by *life as it really is*?" as though I am claiming some special insight into a very complicated phenomenon. Well, the answer is so simple that you might ask why I didn't write it down on a single sheet of paper and pass it around, instead of writing the book! But remember, that when you read these conclusions, there are only two ways. We can choose to enjoy life in the present, or we can allow ourselves to live in dissatisfaction and pain.

This is the view of life as it is, which personal and Living Meditation give us:

1. We all have to live in the present because there is no past or future.
2. We can live in a state of dissatisfaction, where what we hope and wish for is different from what actually happens.
3. Acceptance involves wholeheartedly tol-

erance, and lack of attachment, rather than anger and resentment and clinging on.

5. Tolerant attitudes enable us to have ease, calm and enjoyment of the moment.

WHY MEDITATION IS IMPORTANT

You might ask, *Why do I have to go through the rigmarole of meditation, when I can be happy if I follow your conclusions and become tolerant and kindly?* This is a key question. And the answer is that even if you're an extraordinary sort of person, you'll only keep the conclusions in mind some of the time. Left to ourselves, we tend to be selectively tolerant and kindly. We *choose* the people and situations where we're prepared to show these qualities, and rule out others. It's that old ego swelling up again. "I like this, but I don't see why I have to put up with that."

We may already be the kind of person who is

fairly tolerant with our family, our friends and our fellow workers. But when it comes to those people whom we don't know, from a different ethnic background, with all sorts of strange beliefs, or the guy who daubs graffiti on our fence, we become critical, and sometimes very angry.

I explained that acceptance of life and detachment in the present moment means being tolerant, kindly and compassionate, *without any conditions*. We truly accept things as they are. We don't cling on. We don't make qualifications. We look upon each event that upsets us as a teacher. We learned something. Maybe we learned that it would have been easier all round if we had been a little kinder, a little calmer, a little more detached.

But next time, we'll remember the lesson. As we weather the storms with calm and detachment, we become more and more able to do so. We become more capable of enjoyment.

OK, OK, I know you're thinking, *What about those situations I can't accept, where I should step in and try to make changes?* There are plenty of these.

The son of our neighbour was being bullied at school. It was serious. Kerry's attitude to school had turned to fear and dislike. He was miserable. His mother and father were worried. The mother, Dorothy, said to me, "We've got a choice. We can endure this for a while, go on worrying, in the hope that the school deals with the problem or it goes away, or wade in with a complaint, and a demand for action. Either way is going to be hellish!" It's real life, isn't it? Nothing can take away the fact that we have to use our judgement in these day-to-day problems. As Dorothy could clearly see, both ways open to her and her husband Jack were unpleasant. In the end, they had a meeting with the headmaster. The most they could do to ease the way they had chosen was to be calm about it. Their approach worked, but it might have failed, it might have stirred up issues around Kerry, and other students and their parents. And Dorothy and Jack might have had to say to themselves, "We did the wrong thing here, we should have kept quiet." But even if they had done the wrong thing, the important point was to realise it calmly, and try something else.

When we can take action in more ways than one, Living Meditation can help us with how we go, and it can help us handle our mistakes – we all make them. So acceptance doesn't mean we roll over, and take any punishment handed out to us. It means that we'll approach the problem factually. It's so much less wearing! It means we'll accept, in the case of bullying, that bullying happens, and that our anger isn't going to help resolve it. We won't lose time personalising animosity toward teachers, or other parents whom we think have let us down. In Living Meditation, this problem will probably cost us a lot less anxiety than it otherwise would, because we'll handle it coolly.

There will be many other intimate situations, particularly concerning our relatives and friends, where we have to ask ourselves the serious question whether we can accept what has happened. We'll feel we have to *do* something, to intervene. We'll need to look at the anger, the grief, the envy, the jealousy, which might be generated by a certain line of approach, and see whether they are useful, helpful thoughts, and whether they justify the action we could take. Often, we'll find all we're proposing to do is protect our ego. We're going to make a fuss because we think a fuss is justified, and we want other people to see it. This is the gray path.

There will also be times when we may find that, if we don't act, some harm may come to us, or our family or friends. These are the cases where we have to stand up for ourselves. But in Living Meditation our approach will still remain one of *accepting* that something outside our control has happened. We will appreciate that the key is how we react. And we will refuse to add to our burden by taking on useless emotions like anger. We can see that anger is never *justified*, however bad the scene, simply because it gets us nowhere, makes us look a fool, and most important, adds to our anguish. Every angry moment we have is misery.

A colleague of mine, a clever man, decided to take legal action against a building contractor who made a mess of expensive alterations to his house. Gerry certainly had a case, but he decided to conduct it himself, without a lawyer. He had a great grasp of the very detailed facts, and was smart enough to understand court procedures. The proceedings went on for nearly two years. Gerry was obsessed with them. He always brought up the subject when I talked to him. I think he fought every point in his sleep as well as in court. The case worried him, and hung over him like a black cloud. He eventually won, and bought me a drink on the proceeds. "Was it all worth it?" I asked him. At first, he puffed out his chest at his famous victory, and then admitted, "I wouldn't do it again." Gerry could see that he wasn't just arguing a fair case and winning points. He was conducting a war, a vendetta; he had carried an emotional burden of animosity for two years. It was so unnecessary. He could have used a lawyer. It would have cost more in monetary terms, but saved a fortune in anxiety.

In Living Meditation we seek to approach disputes with the same dispassionate attitude that a lawyer has, and if we can't achieve that, it makes sense to get the help of somebody else who can. There may be a lot of situations, other than lawsuits, where we should get a friend or agent to act, realising how difficult it is to be dispassionate. But for the dozen events that happen every day of the week, and make us depressed and annoyed, the big issue about *whether we can* or *should accept* doesn't arise. We *have* to show acceptance, or be miserable. Somebody is rude to us; we get short-changed at a newsvendor's; a car is blocking our drive; the airline ticket we were promised hasn't arrived; our neighbour never scoops up his dog's poo; our daughter is suddenly ill; the new shoes that cost a fortune pinch our toes; we've had a misunderstanding with our husband; and so it goes on and on. Everyday life. We can wallow in a gray fog of dissatisfaction, or we can accept and walk on.

The kind of acceptance I'm talking of isn't an easy everyday achievement, like trying to be nice. It takes work and training of personal and Living Meditation. If we decide to run three miles a day, at first it's very tough. We sweat and ache. We feel tired afterwards. But after six weeks, we jog rhythmically. Our aches are gone. Instead of feeling tired afterwards, we feel bright. If we stop for a week or ten days, our performance slips back. When we start running again, after a lapse, it's an effort at first to regain that springy feeling of ease. It's like this with the exercise of meditation, and the feeling of calm and acceptance which flows from it.

If we practice consistently our mind muscles are strong. We can gain peace and calm in our actual practice more readily. And we can go on to our day with renewed peace of mind. We renew that peace of mind with every meditation. We can recognise more easily the situations in the day when we have to choose the helpful course of acceptance, rather than the unhelpful one which leads to disappoint-ment, dissatisfaction, irritation and anger – the white path or the gray path. We become very conscious of these moments of choice. We're literally balancing on a wave like a surfer, delicately navigating our board. All day and every day. And with this balance comes calm enjoyment. We need constant practice to do this.

Just as the runner or surfer loses fitness by

not practising, so our ability to achieve calm reduces. Unless we practice, we lose our perspective on true acceptance, and we don't enjoy the moment so much. The "strength" we build up in practice is what we need in order to enjoy life. Personal and Living Meditation are the tools.